COURAGE
Freedom
Happiness

Life Hacks from a Digital Nomad

*Larry,
Come on an adventure with me!*
— Janet

JANET ROUSS
Foreword by Greg Caplan, Founder of Remote Year

© Copyright 2018 Innovation Network Inc. All rights reserved. No portion of this book may be reproduced mechanically, electronically, or by any other means, including photocopying, without written permission of the publisher. It is illegal to copy this book, post it to a website, or distribute it by any other means without permission from the publisher.

ISBN: 978-1-7752714-0-6
Innovation Network Inc.
Toronto, ON Canada M4E 1Z9
www.nicelife.ca

Published in Canada

Dedication

This book is dedicated to those that get out and live.

To all the Remotes who shared the journey. I honor each of yours as I hope you honor mine. To Claire and Gianni, without whom we would not have been Ikigai.

To my friends and family who spurred me on – those that believed I could not only take the journey but supported me while I relived it through these pages.

To Sakura, a stranger from Australia who came along at just the right time to hold me accountable every day for the weeks it took me to write the first draft.

To my friends who proofread the countless final versions of this book to get it as close to perfect as possible.

To my author friends and clients who inspired and encouraged me over the years.

To my book writing club ... I finally finished one!

CONTENTS

Dedication	iii
Foreword	vii
Introduction: Join the Journey	1
PreRemote: Prepare for Take-off	7
Month 1: Party Like it's 1999	12
Month 2: Get Comfortable with the Uncomfortable	32
Month 3: Creativity and the Count	53
Month 4: Road Trips and Romance	70
Month 5: It's Christmas, it Must be Prague	85
Month 6: Rain in Spain Turns to Ice	95
Month 7: Magical Mexico	109
Month 8: Colombian Coffee is the Cure	119
Month 9: City of Eternal Spring	133
Month 10: The Full Monthy	147
Month 11: Nose to the Grindstone	167
Month 12: Dead of Winter at 25°C	179
What's Next?	184
Author's Resources	188

Foreword

COURAGE FREEDOM HAPPINESS – Life Hacks from a Digital Nomad is a very personal journey on a Remote Year 12-month program. It's the first book of its kind to capture the good, the bad and the beautiful of working and traveling with a group to a new city every month.

I first met Janet when her group kicked off their Remote Year journey in Lisbon. I try to meet with as many "Remotes" as I can in person because Remote Year is all about human connections and community.

She was full of life and wide-eyed wonderment, though a little distraught about missing the cable for her newly purchased camera. I was surprised to discover that she was the second oldest Remote in our programs at that time. Her 25 years as a Creative Director in the advertising business must keep her young at heart!

As an international professional speaker, she's traveled to many exotic destinations around the world, so I was honored that she chose to join one of our Remote Year programs.

Janet's vivid memoirs will lure you along her hilarious, and sometimes haunting, descriptions of daily life on the road. You'll want to hang on at every turn.

Her practical and insightful tips for travel preparation, self-care, socializing, working and seeing it all are artfully placed throughout the narrative. Janet's carefully gathered resources to offer you her perspective on what you need to get started down a similar path.

Janet's energy and constant drive to learn, experience and teach makes her an inspiration to adventurers of all ages and life stages. Her life experience brings a confident and courageous perspective to the journey.

I'm truly excited about her book – a must read for anyone who is considering a program specifically focused on working while travelling.

Naturally, I personally recommend Remote Year!

Greg Caplan
Founder / CEO of Remote Year

Introduction: Join the Journey

Destination: Europe, Africa and the Americas

Imagine yourself anywhere in the world doing what you do best — working on your career, practicing your art, studying a new skill or writing a cool travel blog. Whatever you can imagine, you can create. All you need is a dream. Travel with this digital nomad for a year to four continents, 22 countries and too many cities to count, and see how dreams can come true.

"How are you going to top that one?" asked my friend Harry, after I had just come back from a month of working as a Marketing Director at a bank in Riyadh, Saudi Arabia. At the time I had no idea, nor did I even want to.

It was mid-April the following year, and I was speaking on a panel at our professional speakers association in Ottawa, when at lunch something magical happened — literally. I was chatting with the MC for the day. His name was Majid, 'like magic' he would say to help people remember it. As I said, magical.

In the middle of our casual conversation, he asked, "So what do you do in your business?"

Instead of giving my pat answer, something eloquently phrased and crafted to make my branding and marketing offer sound enticing, I just looked deeply into his big brown eyes and said, "All I really want to do is work and travel."

His response was quick, and struck my wanderlust nerve with precision. "Have you heard about Remote Year*?" My eyebrows shot through the roof. "No, what's that?" He proceeded to drop a bomb that blew my whole world apart. An innocent conversation started a domino effect of change.

The next day, Majid had forwarded the Remote Year link. Within two weeks I had applied, was interviewed and offered a spot on the Ikigai itinerary leaving at the end of July. That was in three months!

Remote Year, RY for short, is a small community of digital nomads who travel the world for a year, living in a new city each month. This travel concierge service charges a monthly fee that covers the cost of accommodations, workspaces, internet connection, local experiences and group travel between each city. Just bring your own work, an open mind and desire to see the world.

WHAT ARE YOU AFRAID OF?

"How irresponsible! What if you lose your clients? You can't afford this. What about your son and parents? What about your house?" That gremlin voice is a persistent-little-persnickety-bitch, but more often than not she has a point. I had just enough time to do my due diligence, when the phone rang.

It was Dan, the Remote Year interviewer. There were only two spots left on the Ikigai itinerary (the one that had most of my bucket list places and avoided Asia with that 12-hour time difference.) Perhaps it was just a smooth closing technique, but I wasn't going to take any chances, so I summoned up the courage and charged the non-refundable US$5000 deposit to my credit card.

Literally the day after making that courageous financial commitment to the year, I was meeting with my main client — the one I had worked with for years, the one who loyally retained my monthly services and the one who always paid in less then 30 days. The best client I could ever ask for. The one who would make it possible for me to do this.

Alas, it was the same client who explained to me that very day that their non-essential budgets were being reallocated to the new clubhouse renovations and they would no longer need my services.

It was in that moment, I realized that COURAGE was not about the decision to go. It was about the decision to go after this serious setback.

It was then that the three main qualities of human need started to emerge – **COURAGE FREEDOM HAPPINESS.**

COURAGE roared like a lion with my decision to go. Then it continued to rise up in sometimes terrifying ways at different times throughout the year. The lack of courage is cowardice; the excess of courage is recklessness. The key is finding the balance.

WHAT'S HOLDING YOU BACK?

Being a single mom with a career in the advertising industry kept me busy for 25 years. My son had just flown the coop, so my nest was empty. My parents had just moved out of the house they had lived in for 58 years and settled safely into a lovely retirement apartment.

I always imagined I would retire early and spend my time traveling, but life had other plans. There was never the time, the money or the right person to do it with.

A window of opportunity was opening here. No more childrearing, not yet needed for serious senior care — FREEDOM was banging my damn door down. All I needed was my own permission to start checking things off my bucket list. Maybe there is no perfect time but — this was MY time!

FREEDOM — *The fundamental human right to think, to speak or to act the way we want without restriction — self-imposed or otherwise. Freedom shows up in our lives in many different ways, and once you get a taste of it, it becomes addictive.*

Traveling is a great way to free up your life and create some space to think about what's next. Perhaps this year would reveal some higher knowing, some inner realization or clearer direction for the next stage of my life.

During the year, many of us asked ourselves the same questions. "What will this year bring?" or "What the *&#%* is this all about?" "What is the answer to remote life?" Would there be a payout at the end — a new career, a new love or a new life?

After all, our Remote Year group was called Ikigai. (The term is made up of two Japanese words: ikiru – "to live" and kai – "realize your hopes". So Ikigai suggests your purpose in life or your reason to live.) If we didn't find our Ikigai, would that mean we'd failed? Or at least failed to live up to our name? How would this year change us? What would be different when we got home — if we decided to go home at all?

WHAT MORE COULD YOU WANT?

To some this Remote Year would be a dream come true — excitement, adventure and a sense of FREEDOM beyond imagination. To others it would be a nightmare — constant change, endless challenges and a sense of falling with nothing to hold on to.

It certainly was a wicked, wild rollercoaster ride for the not-so-faint-at-heart. Through all the ups and downs I discovered HAPPINESS.

HAPPINESS — but not in the way you might think. I wasn't searching for happiness. Instead, happiness became my #1 survival skill throughout the year. You'll have to read on to find out how.

At the end of the year, some Ikigais were still traveling, extending their remote work as long as possible. But those of us who came back to our 'normal' lives seemed to be having a similar reaction. There was no A-HA moment, no magical insight, and no golden nuggets of wisdom that naturally emerged.

I started to feel as if it hadn't really happened, that it was just a gap in time that ended right back where I started. What was worse — the memories started to fade, to be covered over with other, more recent memories. The visceral feelings that made the trips so vivid had lost their potency.

So I started to write — memoir-style, just to have a personal record. Who knows, maybe there was a legacy to be left. I began with fervor at the middle of December with the intention of publishing the book by the end of February.

Tight deadlines provide the ultimate creative tension, a perfect balance of anxiety and productivity. Just enough time to get it done and not enough time to stop and think about it.

Over the next month, this book evolved to not only tell the epic tales of Remote Year and all the cool places we went, but also to include my **Life Hacks** — remote or otherwise.

COURAGE, FREEDOM AND HAPPINESS are only a few of the **Life Hacks** which extend beyond travel. They can be applied to any aspect of your life. My stories will show you how these life hacks emerged and how I used them along the way.

My wish is that you will not only join me on this Remote Year, but feel you are a part of it. Whether you are inspired to travel with a group or forge out on your own, I encourage you to use the Life Hacks and check out the resources at the back of the book. Then, please keep me posted on your expeditions!

It would be truly rewarding if I could motivate just one person to have the COURAGE to step through their fears, the FREEDOM to make their own choices and to find the HAPPINESS that is available to them every moment of every day.

This book is a personal journey with stories – some funny and some not-so-much – and Life Hacks for living.

This book is not a complete reference for travel like Frommers or Lonely Planet, nor an objective account of a travel experience.

This is my story. Please enjoy it for all it is.

Bon Voyage.

Janet

PreRemote: Prepare for Take-off

Destination: Home – wherever that may be.

Take stock of what you have, then figure out how much you can fit into a 23 kg suitcase. Now get rid of the rest. Letting go is a practice that takes time. Start with the easy stuff. Slowly but surely minimalize your life. Focus only on the things that are truly meaningful. Feel the FREEDOM in the empty space that is left behind. Unclutter your life — then get packing.

In the flurry of activity that followed from early May to my departure date at the end of July, I wrote lists. I had lists for my lists with sub-lists for minutia.

A list of what I wanted to take. A list of what I wanted to store. A list of what I wanted to sell. A list of what I wanted to give away and to whom. A list of things I needed to do before I left — visas and banking and address changes and and and — the list(s) go on.

There's a blog about my lists on medium.com/@janetrouss

GET PACKING

At the time I discovered Remote Year I was just about to replace all the hardwood floors in my home. After living in the same house for 25 years this was no small feat.

I've been fairly diligent with 'thinning out' on a fairly regular basis. But regardless of how much of a minimalist you aspire to be, there is still a whole lot more stuff than you think tucked away in little corners, under stairs and neatly organized shelves.

The timing was impeccable. I would rent my house out while I was away, so it had to be emptied out anyway. Replacing the floors was like a trial run. The new floors would also fetch a higher rent, and hopefully some awesome tenants.

Before taking off, I had to downsize. This part of the journey requires a lot of COURAGE.

Life Hack: Letting go takes B.A.L.L.S.

Letting go of all of your worldly possessions could make some people completely lose their shit. Our attachment to things can cause a lot of stress when it comes time to moving on. Some things have true sentimental value but other stuff we simply tolerate or keep out of guilt. You know all of those things that you were going to use some day — it's time to get rid of them.

Pierrette Raymond of "Let go. Move Forward. Live Fully." created this great acronym, B.A.L.L.S., to help you make some decisions about changing up your lifestyle and downsizing your stuff. First, it's important to have a vision of your future life. Without some type of criteria it's pretty hard to make choices. Here are some to consider

- **Budget:** *How much are you prepared to spend to hire help, store your stuff or pay to get rid of it? Is there any potential to make money in the process?*
- **Amenities:** *What do you absolutely need to take with you? What amenities will the place where you are staying have?*
- **Lifestyle:** *What do you plan to do while you're away? What clothes and gear will you need to live the lifestyle you envision?*
- **Location:** *Consider the climate and the seasonal changes, the culture and acceptable dress.*
- **Space:** *How much space do you have in your suitcase or pack? How much space will you have where you are going?*

PREPARE TO BE FLEXIBLE

Slowly but surely, between contractors, deliveries and general mayhem, I scratched things off my lists. In my tiny, jam-packed, plastic-tented basement, I lived through six weeks of turmoil – demolition, new sub-floors, leveling and finally the brand new shiny, perfect floor.

I celebrated my first night back in my own bedroom with a nice long, soothing soak in my "deep and delish" bathtub.

After my long luxurious lather, I headed for bed, my mind spinning with all the things that needed to be done in the next month. Sleep evaded me, so I went down to the kitchen for a little bedtime temptation.

At the bottom of the stairs I turned the corner to admire my shiny new floors. I detected a glimmer of light in the darkness. The next step stopped me in my tracks.

The shine was not from the newness of the floor but from the wetness of my bathwater, which had somehow made its way down through the dining room light fixture and showered unforgivingly all over my brand new hardwood floors.

Thank heavens for midnight cravings!

Flipping on the light, I was shocked that the new solid maple boards were already starting to swell at the ends. I did what I could to stop the water damage.

I panicked and paced in the way one does in the early hours of the morning. With no-one to call, no way to vent, tears welled up and poured like torrents of bathwater down my cheeks.

You know those times when you feel you're being tested? Well this was certainly one of them. I've passed many of these tests and much greater ones in my life, so I was determined to deal with this and move on.

I sopped up all the water, cranked the fan on high and decided to deal with the rest in the morning. I went back to bed exhausted and in shock. I'd lost my appetite for a snack.

Emotional Hack

Emotional resilience is the ability to bounce back or let things roll off you. It certainly helps if you improve your emotional resilience before heading off or taking on something that seriously stretches you outside your comfort zone.

Next time you face a difficult situation, try to sit with the discomfort. It's okay to be in turmoil — this too shall pass. Don't be rash in your decisions — gain some perspective first.

Perspective comes with time. Let go of having all the right answers and practice accepting things just the way they are. This is part of the path to true HAPPINESS.

I eventually settled back to relatively normal living by the end of June. Dealing with the aftermath of the big bathwater barrage was just one of the many things on my many lists in preparation for my Remote Year.

The last month went by in a nausea-inducing flurry of non-stop multi-tasking. As I slowly packed up my home, my world became smaller and smaller. I was funneling everything I owned through these filters:

1) Store it, 2) Lend it, 3) Dump it and 4) Take it.

By the end of July, there were only a few things I thought I would need for the year. They seemed small relative to my house and what I had already packed away, but when I tried to fit them to a 23kg suitcase, those piles were enormous!

Pack Hack

Don't pack anything you haven't used in the past week. You can buy pretty much anything where you are going. You don't need full size products of any kind. Once you've decided what to take — reduce it by half. Then reduce that by half again. That's probably all you'll need. Seriously! This hack was confirmed by many of my fellow Ikigais.

Through the process of elimination, I slowly but surely whittled my belongings down to fit into that 23kg suitcase, a rolling carryon and my trusty backpack. It was fascinating to see that I packed the same amount for a year away as I did for a week's vacation.

Remember I told you about those lists? Well I finally did scratch the last thing off. Departure day had finally arrived. As my plane lifted off, the stress and anxiety of those last three months remained on the tarmac as gravity pressed my body into Seat 38A on Air Canada flight #856 bound for Lisbon.

Month 1: Party Like it's 1999

Destination: Portugal – Lisbon and beyond ~ August

Prince is one of my all-time favourite artists. His music brings me HAPPINESS. His song '1999' was released in 1983 when I was 24 years old, the same age as most of the people I'm traveling with. In fact, I'm probably the same age as most of their parents, which I'm pretty sure created just as much tension as connection. It's summertime in Lisbon – let's get the party started!

Arriving at Lisbon airport, I was met by our Remote Year program leader, Claire, who would travel with us for the entire year. I loved her the minute I met her, and the warmth of her welcome immediately confirmed that I had done the right thing.

We were whisked away to our accommodations: two student dorms known as uHub and 9SL. I was in uHub, where we had individual contemporary rooms, each with a bed, balcony and lots of closet space — rather ironic considering my minimal luggage. My room had a little kitchenette, which was wonderful. HAPPINESS was making it my home for the first month.

In uHub there was a common area on the roof, with a huge kitchen where we could prepare larger meals, gather for our social events and work if we didn't want to walk to the co-working space.

The Rooster of Barcelos says, "See the Lisbon office video and other cool stuff from the journey at NiceLife.ca."

Arrival Hack

It's important to settle into your space when you arrive in a new place. If you are staying for longer than a week, take the time to unpack right away and put things away where you know you can find them. Take stock of what is in the kitchen and what you need to make your daily life more comfortable. Simple things keep us grounded — salt and pepper, a fry pan, a dish brush — it may seem silly but common items can be calming.

The sooner you can call the place home, the sooner you'll be able to roam without feeling too uprooted.

Make a list of your basic necessities so that you can check off what's there, and fetch whatever you still need on your first outing. Make this outing a tour of the neighbourhood to become familiar with your local green grocer, butcher and convenience store.

Stock up your fridge so that you'll have supplies when you come home later. Try new foods, but keep some of your regular staples so your tummy doesn't act up. You don't want that slowing you down.

LET'S GET ORIENTED

The orientation day at the co-working space was a great way to get to know the other Remotes. We each had a chance to share what we could offer the group and what we were hoping to get in return.

We set the norms for the group: respect, no judgment, curiosity, kindness, support, etc. — all the things we wanted to hold people accountable for. Everyone seemed to be on the same page, which was reassuring.

Group Hack

*I learned this valuable principle as a college instructor and was thrilled to see it in action with our Remote Year group. We all have a slightly different interpretation of values. For example, **fun** for one person is very different than **fun** for another.*

When travelling with a group it's important to set some rules for everyone to follow. Have each individual agree to follow those rules and hold people accountable if they don't.

Our welcome dinner at the funky Village Underground venue, behind the LX Factory in a refurbished industrial part of town under the massive bridge, was an awesome way to start the month.

Another evening event early on was at the revived Pensaō Amor — Guesthouse of Love, in other words an old city brothel! This was located in the former red light district, now literally painted and called the Pink Street.

It was exciting to have a night out with the other Remotes at this bordello chic spot, where the burlesque stage held café tables occupied by an eclectic mix of artists, beatniks and tourists. I was feeling young again!

My futile attempts to be last one standing, however, failed miserably — I was out of practice. Night after night, try as I might, I simply couldn't keep up.

It wasn't long before I threw up the white flag in surrender. Staying out late and having that extra drink seemed like a good idea at the time, but my recovery was slow and I had places to go.

There are many hidden treasures in Portugal I needed to explore. I couldn't afford to lose days and nights in an effort to keep up with the young'uns. I made a choice — to take care of myself and make the most of my time.

Selfcare Hack

Everyone has a different tolerance and recovery level. Listen to your body and heed its warning. As tempting as it is to go full out, it will only lead to burnout if you don't take care of yourself. Selfcare is one of the top life hacks, and all the Ikigais agreed, to sustain a healthy and long digital nomad life.

RELATIONSHIPS

Our first month was like a honeymoon, with everyone so excited, so interested and eager to make friends. The seeds of romances were being planted and the first round of tryouts had begun. It was interesting to watch without participating — providing advice from the sidelines and wagering on who would end up with whom.

There were two couples who came on the trip together. There was the lovely Nandita, a brain scientist, and her husband Ankor, a business consultant from India. The other couple, Becca and Jacob, were both UX (User Experience) designers from New York City. Both couples were solid and weathered the journey well.

Then there were the married folks who came solo, like Hilary B, Melissa G., and Mikko, along with others who left their boyfriends or girlfriends at home while they romped around the world. Some of those relationships worked with occasional visits, other not so much.

It's a big risk to put your relationship on hold for an entire year — especially if it's already a little rocky. Chances are some of them were already looking for an out when they left. Traveling opens you up to all sorts of opportunity.

Whether it was losing a job, a partner, a business or moving on to a new stage in life, it seemed many participants were propelled into Remote Year by some life-changing event.

GROUP DYNAMICS

It's intriguing to see what happens when you put 70+ strong-willed individuals in the same situation. You know what it feels like when you walk into a room and you are instantly drawn to certain people as if there is an etheric magnet pulling you closer? Those are the people you bond with — maybe even for life.

Then there are others who have the opposite effect. You don't even see them, or maybe you're even a little repulsed. No matter what you try to do, those folks will never be part of your inner circle — and that's okay. These dynamics played out in subtle and not-so-subtle ways in our first month and throughout the year.

Although overall as a group we were pretty inclusive, some individuals made quick work of forming tight-knit connections. The beautiful thing about doing this type of trip is that those relationships will often last a lifetime.

Due to the generation gap, I sometimes felt I missed out on the intensity of those relationships but still walked away at the end with great and lasting friendships.

IT'S EASY TO FIND TRAVEL COMPANIONS

The great thing about traveling with travelers is that they don't take much convincing to join you in a side trip. Back at home in the midst of those renos, I had already arranged a side trip to one of my bucket list places — Porto, the positively charming town known for its namesake, port wine.

I extended the invitation in our Ikigai Facebook group, and over 30 Remotes decided to come along for the weekend. It was fabulous — another great opportunity to bond and sample the elixir of life. I checked the first place off my bucket list – sipping port at Taylor Fladgate with my new friends while overlooking the town of Porto.

We sipped port, toured the city and dined at the fabulous A Tasquinha restaurant. That weekend would mark the first of our yearlong tradition of Sunday Fun Day brunches. This one was at Cervejaria Brasão and included the famous local Francesinha, or little Frenchie sandwich, that originated in Porto. A cacophony of meats piled high inside two pieces of white bread covered in a hot, thick tomato and beer sauce served with french fries — the perfect hangover cure.

And I badly needed that, since the Porto pulse had invigorated me so much I had a late night on the dance floor. Some liquid courage gave me the FREEDOM to pull out a few of my famous belly dancing moves. For those who were still tentative about the old gal, this firmly cemented my position as a night club contender, as I would discover later that month during the slideshow at our Farewell Lisbon party.

That night also revealed my alter ego, Juanita, the fun party gal who doesn't get out much but when she does — watch out! Eventually most of the Remotes would have similar alternative personality names emerge as the night and the libations wore on.

Social Hack

If you find yourself traveling over a long period of time with a group, focus on what you have in common, not what makes you different. If you're struggling, then ask yourself, "How might I find a common interest?"

When you position social challenges as a potential as opposed to a problem, your brain will look for ways to fill in that void.

Stay positive and compassionate. Relationships you may never have considered can open up an entirely new world. Open-mindedness is essential when you travel due to the variety in cultural, generational and gender norms around the world.

You are here to discover, so don't try to fit everything into your comfortable box. Don't look for other people to make you happy. Your HAPPINESS attracts the right people to you.

Be ready to embrace difference and release judgment around things and people you don't understand.

TIME TO WORK

It was tough to work with all the allure of local destinations and the expanding splinter group side trips. But I had bigger issues to resolve. I needed to gather the COURAGE to make some headway with new business development to replace the income I had just lost with my main client.

The fact that it was August, the height of summer vacation time, made it hard to reach people, and when I did, everything was pushed off to September. Thank goodness I had the rental income to cover my expenses and some savings for my daily spending.

I probably spent more time than I should have on social media — posting pictures and stories of my first month's escapades. But then something miraculous happened — referrals came pouring in.

People who knew me back home were starting to notice my Facebook posts. They were curious and inspired about where I was and what I was doing. The word got out that I was "living the dream" — the entrepreneur's fantasy of running a business remotely while traveling the world.

Apparently I had found the Holy Grail. People wanted to work with me in the hope that some of that magical power would rub off on them, so I got busy with conversations that converted to clients. Securing those September starts gave me the freedom to explore more of Portugal — and check off a few more places on my bucket list.

Remote Working Hack

If you are seriously considering taking your business on the road, check out the author references in the back of this book. I also provide tips, or hacks, throughout the chapters that you might find helpful.

Remember Dan, that guy who interviewed me for Remote Year? He now coaches people on how to convince their employers to let them work remotely. His contact details are in the Author Resources at the back of the book.

There was a wide spectrum of work styles and ethics amongst my fellow Remotes — from sales people to full stack developers, from human resource specialists to fitness instructors.

Some had dedicated nine-to-five jobs, working diligently to prove to their employers they made the right decision by letting them take this year to travel and work.

Others were clinging halfheartedly to jobs they hated, hoping the year would re-inspire them or find them a new direction. Others, like me, ran their own businesses or worked as freelancers to keep their dream alive.

Then there were the people in 'transition' who had the FREEDOM to reinvent themselves or just floating along for the ride — looking for their Ikigai. They certainly joined the right group.

WE ARE IKIGAI

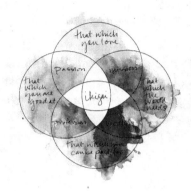

The Japanese concept of ikigai refers to the thing that gives your life meaning. It's at the core of what you do well, what you like to do, what the world needs and what you can get paid for — that is your ikigai.

It's the thing that gets you up every morning — your purpose, your passion, your pleasure. "Ikigai or Die!" became our battle cry. We were a force together and strong soldiers apart.

I had never really traveled with a group before, so I was happy they were there — but just as happy to know I could come and go as I pleased. And come and go I did.

POSEIDON'S PRIDE

When I was in my early 20s, I used to hang with my friend Terry. She is Portuguese and passionate about sardines. Seriously! Her father used to buy them fresh and BBQ them in their backyard. It was a traditional Portuguese barbecue with all the fixings, and Terry was an award-winning chef, so you know that we ate the best. Ever since then, Portugal has been on my bucket list, but I never really appreciated that passion for sardines until I came to Lisbon.

In Lisbon, the artisan food culture is alive and well in the canned fish world. There are countless canneries whose sole (pun intended) purpose is to pack little tins with their Poseidon's pride and joy. Their works of art can be purchased at any number of speciality shops, like the historic Conserveira de Lisboa or Loja das Conservas, the outlet for the National Association of Canned Fish Industry, which promotes products from fish canneries throughout Portugal and its outer islands.

Let me also introduce you to Miss Can, a simple fisherman's wife who had the COURAGE to create one of the sexiest sardine shops in Lisbon, near São Jorge Castle.

Since opening in 2013, Miss Can has won the National Prize for Creative Industries (PNIC) in Portugal and Arla Foods Innovation Challenge in Creative Business Cup in Copenhagen — what a tremendous achievement.

I was surprised by my obsession with sardines, which was not shared by many of the other Remotes. As I would find out, they preferred a more 'American' diet.

If you don't love the sultry sardine, then Time Out Market will be more up your alley. This giant building is part of the adjacent farmers market, that caters more to tourists and trendy locals it has evolved into an open-seating central hall where high-end restaurateurs serve up their sweet and savoury fare in food-court-style stalls around the outside. They tempt you with tasty dishes to entice you to come to their more established restaurants in other parts of the city.

I juggled my client projects so that I could explore the city — sometimes during the day and other times at night when the sun was too hot, sometimes on my own and sometimes with other like-minded Remotes. There is so much to see and do in Lisbon.

Daily Hack

Many travelers bring their Uber-use along with them, although several countries have banned the business or have made it very difficult or downright dangerous to drive.

Why not dive into the city transit system? Wrap your head around the closest entry point to underground Metro stations and surface transit stops. Then use your Google Maps to navigate to where you want to go. Pick a random place far away so you discover different parts of the city.

Make your way to a suburban mall if that makes you happy. Lisbon's transit system includes the ferries that go across the river. Buying a transit pass could save you a lot of money.

LOVE THOSE TILES

Portugal is known for its ceramic arts. Even the Metro stations have incredible displays of art. (For those interior designers in the crowd, it gives a whole new meaning to the term "subway tile".)

Decorative tiles, known as azulejos, are also used on the buildings as a way of controlling the temperature by deflecting the sun in the summer and keeping in the heat in the winter.

The tile museum is definitely worth a visit, or you may get your fill just walking around the city. The bairos (neighbourhoods) are fascinating, especially the Bairo Alto area. Make sure you are in good shape because some of those hills are a pretty steep.

The waterfront is refreshing and the government buildings beautiful. The central shopping streets tend to be touristy but well worth a wander. Make sure you hop on the old fashioned Tram 28. Just watch for pickpockets while you ride it through the main part of town to the São Jorge Castle — a must see.

I was shocked at how quickly the first month had gone by. It was the last weekend and the end of my love affair with Lisbon was looming. Other than Porto, I had not ventured beyond the hilly walks around Lisbon, and there was still so much to see.

I wanted to visit Sintra and take a weekend road trip to a few neighbouring beach towns. Try as I might, though, I couldn't find anyone to join me. Aborting my plans would feel like the ultimate rejection, so it was clear I was going alone — because going alone is better than not going at all.

It took a while to summon up the COURAGE to book the car and go. I finally just did it.

Google guided me to the pick-up location. Sans human navigation, the car's GPS kept me on track. Off I went down along the Costa da Caparica coastline to Arrabida, where I dipped my toes in the ocean off Setubal and Sesimbra.

As I drove through forests and fields, valleys and vineyards, my love affair expanded through Portugal.

The sun was setting over the west coast and the skies were growing darker. I had one stop left before heading back to uHub for the night. I negotiated the narrow streets of the Alto de Ponte neighbourhood up, up, up — to the majestic statue of Cristo Rei — Christ the King — on the south side of the river, a replica of Christ the Redeemer in Rio de Janeiro.

YOU BE YOU

Next day I headed to the fascinating fairytale town of Sintra, about an hour northwest of Lisbon, where I planned to meet up with a group of Remotes for breakfast.

On my way I took a little detour to pick up some Pastéis de Nata, Portugal's mouth-watering custard tarts, from none other than the original Pastéis de Belem bakery, universally known over a gazillion years for their perfect flaky pastry — oh, that pastry!

After breakfast in Sintra we would ascend the mountain to the colourful Palacio da Pena perched at the top, but not before getting a little lost. It's interesting what happens to a person (like me!) who likes to maintain control.

Let me tell you about the "Right Fight". I was certain that the path up the hill was "this way." Some others insisted it was "that way." My futile attempt to maintain a minuscule sense of control triggered a righteous display of opposition.

Defiant in my position, I persisted — "This way!" After my steadfast righteous opposition, I finally conceded with the group consensus to go "That way." We found the path. I was wrong. I trudged on. Defeated. Rejected. Embarrassed. I apologized.

The long climb up the hill gave me time to reflect on my behaviour. For 25 years, I was a single mom who ran creative departments in the high-demand ad agency world. I've had more than enough personal challenges to deal with in my life. In order to hold myself together, my default is to maintain control — mentally, emotionally and physically.

It made me tough — tough enough to push through barriers, overcome challenges and achieve incredible things in my life. If I put my mind to something, I can pretty much **make** it happen – like this book. But try as I might, I cannot move a path up a mountain!

In one sweaty, shameful moment, it struck me that if I wanted to survive a year of travel with 70 smart, independent individuals, there lay a lesson in letting go. Letting go of control. As I've been travelling solo since I was 24 years old, it would be perhaps one of the hardest lessons for me to learn.

A lifetime of control had brought me to this point. How could I let go when control was my friend, my colleague, my support and trusted advisor? It gave me a sense of leadership, composure, calmness, self-restraint. It provided boundaries, rules, limitations and safety. All good things, right? Yes, but there is also FREEDOM in being a follower.

Social Hack

Lack of control does not necessarily mean mayhem. Relinquishing control is a way of building trust in others.

In the extreme, the notion of being out of control could conjure up hasty thoughts around abuse or failure. However, letting go of control does not mean losing control.

The opposite of control is simply a choice to let go and let others take the lead while you follow. It's not a novel concept, but it can be a bit hard to practice if it's not your default behavior.

Especially when you are under stress, emotionally vulnerable or outside your comfort zone. Being in control is a survival instinct — the attempt to manage what you can manage when all else is beyond your control.

But when you do surrender control there is a wonderful sense of FREEDOM, allowing you to simply enjoy the moment rather than control it.

FAIRYTALE ENDING

The rest of the climb was spectacular. My inner dialogue soon surrendered to awe as the massive landscape expanded below us with every step up. The Palacio da Pena at the top was a romantic fairytale palace in a Moorish-Romanesque style with multi-coloured sections, housing historical contents from years past.

My visit was shortened by the fact my parking meter was about to run out of time and I had a jam-packed itinerary for that day. So I bid farewell to my friends and headed back down the hill. I was content to reunite with my trusty GPS and find new adventures in the hills beyond Sintra.

PUT ON THE BRAKES!

I discovered something else about myself that day — I derive immense joy from being in ridiculous driving situations!

The road out of Sintra winds around a huge rocky outcrop. Tight as a hairpin, the road also tilts up at a 45-degree angle. On this busy, tourist-filled Saturday the traffic was bumper-to-bumper at a dead stop, while the driver up ahead tried to negotiate around a giant tour bus.

There I sat for an eternity, perched halfway up this serious incline, with cars almost touching both bumpers and gravity pushing me back into my seat. My right foot strained from pushing the brake pedal almost through the floorboard, while my left foot nervously toyed with the clutch. It's been a while since I drove a standard, and creeping up a steep hill was never my favorite thing to do — never mind in a car I hadn't quite got the hang of yet.

It looked as if I would be in that spot for the rest of the day, but the driver up ahead finally made a move and it was time for me to move as well. The car ahead had made significant progress up the hill. Anticipating my move, the driver behind me inched even closer to my tail. As I grasped for the COURAGE to move forward, my blood pumped the warmth of panic through my body as I mentally timed the release of the clutch while flooring the gas.

The screeching and smell of a burning clutch drew attention from all around. As I inched up the hill to my next resting spot just a few meters ahead, I began to laugh. Not a giggle or a chuckle, but an uncontrollable roaring, hooting and howling, ridiculously tear-filled LMAO!

Laughter turned my panic into HAPPINESS. It took me to the top of the mountain and back down the road, where moments later my own face-to-face encounter with another giant tour bus set me off in a laughing fit once again!

The roads around Sintra are pretty much single lanes (I mean one single lane — not a single lane in each direction) with deep gullies on either side. So when one faces an oncoming tour bus there aren't many places to go. I held my breath (as if that would help) and squeezed over to the side — my wheels clinging desperately to the edge of the gutter. The undercarriage hugged the hump on the side of the road, as I prayed there was enough room for the bus to get by.

I waited, blind to what was going on beside me, staring ahead wondering how the hell I would get back up on the road if and when the bus and its oblivious passengers continued down into Sintra. But I soon crawled back up onto the road — laughing uncontrollably as I headed west.

GO TO THE EDGE

FREEDOM took me to my final destination that day, Cabo da Roca, the westernmost tip of continental Europe. Then I drove on to Guincho Beach to watch the kite surfers at sunset while dining on a delicious seafood soup and chunky fries. Life is good.

The weekend road trip was finished off the next day with a visit to the beach with my friend, Melissa G. We savored the hours in the sun before I had to return the car. It was a perfect weekend road trip.

That was my last adventure in Portugal. We were heading to Morocco the next weekend, and I had lots of work to catch up on. I was sad to leave Lisbon. It will always be my first love — but not my last.

LISBON TO RABAT TRAVEL DAY

Transition Day — the true test of COURAGE for any Remote Year program leader. This is the day when everyone must come together and stay together for a transition to the next city. It's a bit like herding cats — especially after rumpus farewell parties in freewheeling drink-all-night-on-the-street Lisbon.

This was our first travel day as a group, and our fearless, faithful and unfettered leader, Claire, was at the helm. All was planned to perfection and executed flawlessly in her head. We were simply to report to the bus at the designated time, reverting to schoolchildren or a tourist mentality. Just show up, get on the bus and everything would be fine.

Everything — until we woke to discover the Lisbon airport security staff had gone on an impromptu strike at 8 am that day. Surprise!! Quick — everyone on the bus NOW!! This was certain to be a cluster f--k. The broken and hurting were hustled out of their beds, while studious folk reported to the bus in minutes.

When we arrived at the airport it was apparent the few hours we saved that morning were not going to make a whole lot of difference. The check-in desk was still only going to open three hours before the scheduled flight. The airport arranged for last minute private security firms and local police, and even flew in security forces from neighbouring Spain to deal with the security inspection.

You can imagine the delays, as security lines screeched to a stop. Frustrated, freaked-out flyers flung their fury as they missed flight after flight departing with barely a soul onboard. We were in seven-hour line-up with nowhere else to go. In line we met people who were trying to board a new flight for the second or third time, having missed their original ones. It would have been impossible to anticipate this ahead of time.

A Plan B might be easier if you were travelling solo, but traveling with a group of this size presents bigger issues. With everyone scattered throughout the queue, there was nothing to do but wait. And wait we did.

I walked the line with Melissa S., the most energetic and animated Remote in the group. I was happy to spend the time with her, as our conversation zigged and zagged like the ropes that finally guided us to the x-ray machines.

While some folks manoeuvred their way to the front quickly, others were caught in the back. Poor Claire was somewhere in the crowd, losing her mind. Talk about losing control! The lesson hits us all at some point, but this is where leaders surrender to followership and followers become leaders.

One such leader was Anu, who surreptitiously snuck her way to the gate and came up with this ingenious plan. If 75 people don't show up to board a small aircraft destined to Morocco, then it's likely the plane won't take off. Especially if we were all checked in. It was a gamble, but the only option we had to ensure everyone traveled together. It worked! Hours late, exhausted and worn thin, we finally landed in Africa.

Travel Hack

Make sure you take physical copies of your passport and keep them in a safe place in case you lose the original.

Using your phone to take a photo of your passport is only a third backup option. If you lose your phone and don't have the pictures backed up, then you've lost your copy, too.

Always keep your passport in the same place, and put it there whenever you are not actually showing it to anyone. Immediately after you show it, put it away — in that same place.

Doing this will save you any blinding panic moments when you can't find it.

Never put your passport in the seat pocket in front of you on a plane.

Lock up your passport at your destination, and keep it there unless you need it for identification purposes at the bank or when buying travel tickets. Check ahead if you are taking side trips, as some accommodations require your passport and entry stamp before check-in.

We finally arrived in Casablanca ... but it wasn't over yet.

Month 2:
Get Comfortable with the Uncomfortable

Destination: Morocco – Rabat, Marrakech, Fez and Chefchauen ~ September

After living in the luxury of western European life, where freedom ruled and drinking in public was encouraged, we entered the mysterious world of Morocco — at the opposite end of the comfort spectrum. It was seductive and scary. It was edgy and expansive. It was hot as hell and the non-stop adventures took a lot of COURAGE.

On arrival, we found that our delay had, in fact, been fortuitous. The group that called Rabat home before us had saved some of their wild shenanigans for travel day, and poor judgment had left several of them unable to travel to their next destination.

Caught up in this sticky situation, our local program leaders were distracted from their welcome duties, so our apartments were not ready to move in. Catered pizza at the co-working space, with little in the way of alcohol to numb the pain, didn't really cut it.

The travel-weary crashed in crumpled piles on various sofas and pillows spread throughout the two-story building and the rooftop lounge area. We were finally ushered to our oppressive old apartment behind the train station at 3 am. This was our home for the next five weeks. The relentless challenge of travel day seemed to seep into the entire month.

GETTING AROUND

The 7AY co-working space was far away from everything, located in an industrial area on the edge of the river. We had to take 'Carems' — the Moroccan version of Ubers — every day. The workspace itself was awesome, though, as were the owners.

The Welcome party on *Le Dhow* ship in the harbour unveiled the eclectic themes yet to come. A traditional Moroccan band and DJ entertained us while we indulged in exotic foods.

Later in the evening, I befriended Ghali, a political advisor to a local TV station. At my insistence, he and his friend took Margit and me to the most popular street food spot in town. I wanted an authentic taste of local life – apparently that included sheep brains, head meat and liver, along with regular ol' chicken.

I wasn't so keen on the texture of the brains and reconfirmed my disdain for liver.

The conversation, however, was enlightening. It was so interesting to discover the historic and current business, cultural and political state of the country. I love hearing it from informed locals — thanks, Ghali.

DISCOMFORT EDGES IN

Morocco is exotic and exciting at its best, but it's also tinged with a droning undercurrent of discomfort. At worst, it's an edge that cuts sharply when you brush up against it.

The edginess may come from the muted sandstorm coating or the mysterious social undercurrent. It was hard to put your finger on it but it saw many of the Remotes flee north to other parts of the Mediterranean to ride out this Moroccan month of mayhem in more conducive locations.

One of my drivers captured this sentiment perfectly. He said, "I hope you take the time to find the beauty in Morocco." The rest of us toughed it out, determined to find that beauty.

Social Hack

If you are not traveling with a group and want a more local experience, the best way to meet the locals is to check out MeetUp.com or Couchsurfing.com. The Couchsurfing community isn't just for accommodations. There is a very active community of people who engage in regular social events, inviting travelers to join and learn more about their city. It's a safe way to meet people, because everyone registers online and there is a two-way feedback that allows everyone to comment on their interaction.

If you want to meet expats (non-locals living abroad) there are dozens of online communities you can join, such as internations.org or expatfinder.com or simply search for Expats (_your country_). You'll find tons of resources on Facebook and LinkedIn too.

NEGOTIATING THE GROCERIES

Much of your remote experience is influenced by the home you have, the neighborhood you live in and the people you room with for that month. I was delighted to spend the month with the lovely and talented designer, Erica Brooks. She made things look simple with her positive, outgoing attitude. It took the edge off venturing out on our first day for a rooftop breakfast and our first shopping trip.

Fetching groceries was an adventure. It felt like a video game with the goal of making it back and forth across a huge traffic circle without getting hit by a constant flow of cars. It was made all the more challenging by the need to haul supplies of drinking water, toilet paper and everything we needed to set up a kitchen for the month. I was almost hit by a beat-up Honda but managed to slip past his bumper just in time. Or perhaps he just timed it that way.

Safety Hack

The key to survival on the streets of Morocco, or any other seemingly chaotic roadway, is to observe the locals and do as they do — walk with purpose. Inside that chaos there is an uncanny respect for those who drive or walk with determination.

Clarity in pacing and direction allows drivers to anticipate your movements and adjust their speed and trajectory accordingly. He who hesitates compromises the flow.

Unloading our market burden would have been a huge relief if it weren't for the stark reality of our kitchen. The apartment was decorated with a mismatched variety of some of the most hideous ceramic tiles I've ever seen.

The kitchen tiles were the worst — a busy weave of brown and beige and blah. To make matters worse, the tiles covered all the walls, the counters **and** the floor!

The kitchen felt like a cell for the criminally insane — not that I have any idea what that would be like. What I do know is that kitchen was a design crime.

YOUR HOME IS YOUR HAVEN

Any hope of making a nice home in this cacophony of colored calamity was lost. We were warned at the beginning of the year that each of us would have a breakdown — hit a wall. My wall was made of poo brown ceramic tiles.

The reality of traveling for **one entire year**, away from the familiar — family, friends and home — hit me like a brick. It would be inevitable, even normal, to crash, and crash I did. Right there in that kitchen in our dark and gloomy apartment in Rabat. It was September, heading into fall, my favourite time of year at home.

It dawned on me that October was just around the corner, and I began to remember how it always was back home. Autumn colours would emerge and my family would gather to celebrate Canadian Thanksgiving and many birthdays including my son, my mother, my niece and nephews, my brother-in-law, along with my best and a host of other friends — and me!

This FOMO was real. I would be missing out on all of it — an entire year away!! What was I thinking?

Emotional Hack

Fear of Missing Out, or FOMO, is a term that emerged with social media that can truly compromise your HAPPINESS. It results in feelings of anxiety or rejection because you perceive others to be having a better time then you.

It happens in everyday life, and even more when you are away from home travelling with a large group. At any given time you will be missing out on something.

To overcome FOMO, make clear personal choices that are in your best interest, and be okay with those choices. If you are confident in your decisions, there is less chance you will succumb to the anxiety of missing out.

Accept the fact that no matter what you are doing, there is always someone doing something else. It's impossible to be in two places at once. You are the only one responsible for your own HAPPINESS. Own it.

Limit your use of social media and spend more time savoring the present moment.

DEALING WITH DISCOMFORT

In the depths of my despair, a drink could have eased the sting of sadness. The bar scene in Rabat is hidden behind blackened windows, as Muslim culture does not condone public displays of drinking.

Gone were the patio cocktails, the cute little bars that served us inside but encouraged patrons to linger on the streets and the rooftop revelry of the Park Lounge back in Lisbon — one of our favourite haunts. Gone. All gone. Stay calm and carry on.

This was the month I would discover the #1 secret to surviving this entire year away. It wasn't about calling home. It wasn't about rallying together with false friends to prop you up or pretending that all was okay.

I searched inside for the answer and was reminded of what the Buddha said, "Pain is inevitable — suffering is optional." It was about consciously choosing and creating my own inner HAPPINESS.

I couldn't deny my emotions. My loneliness and disconnection were real. My emotions were valid. Suppressing them would only make them come out more strongly.

I was not about to abort my yearlong mission, nor was I prepared to wallow in my own pity party. The only thing I had control over was how I reacted to it all.

If I stood stoically in the face of that emotional pain, greeting it like an old friend. That was the only way to make it easier to manage my response to any negative feelings that emerged.

Then I would be compassionate with myself, holding those emotions gently through the hurt. Not beating myself up even more, with comments like "How dare you feel bad, look what you get to do."

It occurred to me that I was going through a mini-loss, and I tried hard to be aware of the process of loss, DABDA – Denial, Anger, Blame, Depression and Acceptance. It was normal to feel these things. But suffer? I don't think so.

HAPPINESS IS A SURVIVAL INSTINCT

It became vividly clear to me that no matter what I do or where I go, I have a choice in every moment to be happy or suffer in relation to the situation or circumstance I find myself in.

I imagined our feelings plotted on an emotional scale from the positive spectrum, working from elation or utter joy through neutral awareness in the middle to sadness and deep depression on the negative end. On any day or in any moment we are triggered by events that send us unconsciously back and forth across that spectrum.

It is up to our conscious minds to decide how long we want to dwell in that spot. We create inner dialogue or stories, and even attract more 'evidence' to reinforce our position; depending on how committed we are to staying in that particular emotional state. I've learned over the years that returning to the centre and maintaining a neutral positive position not only keeps me sane — it makes me happy.

Emotional Hack

Your outlook and attitude, your thoughts, feelings and beliefs, what you say and the actions you take create your reality. You have the freedom every day and in every way to choose happiness.

Denying our emotions is not the route to happiness. Emotions show up to tell us about ourselves. We need to recognize them, be grateful that we have feelings – that's what makes us human. Then let those feelings go.

It's possible to dwell on an emotion and own it to the extent that it becomes a label. For example, you might say, "I'm a jealous person" just because you felt jealousy or I'm an anxious person or I'm an angry person because you identify with those feelings. You could also be attracting people and situations to justify those labels, rather than simply recognizing the emotion and moving on with your life.

Try this out. Next time you become aware of a negative emotion surfacing, try to identify it, give it a name. Is it anger, frustration, loss, etc.? Recognize it for what it is — just a feeling. It does not define you. It's something you are experiencing.

Instead of building on that feeling – creating drama around it or making it part of 'who you are'. Simply validate your feelings. Say, "Thank you 'fear' or 'anger' or 'jealousy'. I hear you and understand your purpose is to protect me. Everything will be okay." Then choose to say goodbye to the feeling and do what you need to do in order to move on.

Like anything, it takes practice. I'll guarantee those feelings will come back time and time again. That's just what emotions do. You may have to repeat this exercise a lot at first to really get the hang of it. If you make this a daily practice, you will notice that your emotions become less intense, less disruptive and subside more quickly.

Doing this increases your Emotional Resilience — the ability to react and recover from normal human emotions in a more effective and efficient manner.

This allows us to continue on with our day in a happier way. Happiness is a mindset, not a state of mind. It's a choice you make every day and in every moment while dealing with an emotional reaction to life.

So there I was in Morocco, feeling sorry for myself. That was a choice I made in one moment, but I didn't intend to stay there. I also could make a choice to release the suffering and look on the bright side.

I was in freakin' Morocco!! OMG!! And we were about to go on an epic desert safari. FREEDOM!!

DESERT ADVENTURE

With my new perspective on life, Morocco became one of the most fascinating of all our remote locations this year.

As much as it harboured the bleak and mysterious, it was also home to the fabulous and fascinating. Again thanks to Anu, over 30 of us were able to participate in an incredible Desert Safari. Though some opted for the five-day version, most of us went for three-days leaving from Marrakech.

That meant I got to ride the fabled Marrakech Express from that old Crosby, Stills & Nash song — all on board the train!! For three intense days, the adventures didn't stop. From souk swindlers to market mongrels, our first night in Marrakech was nothing short of mesmerizing.

Our Marrakech stay was inside the medina – the old historic part of town with high stone walls and very little signage. We stayed in a riad — a traditional Moroccan home with an interior courtyard surrounded by guest rooms. Most riads in the medina are behind non-descript doorways you could never find on your own. These doors open up to magnificent homes, with many rooms and beautiful gardens and/or pools in the centre courtyard.

The incredible Moroccan tile work put my poor kitchen back in Rabat to shame. The giant palm fronds, Arabic archways and majestic furnishings made us feel like royalty. This was the Morocco I had been hoping for. And there was much more!

After a day of walking around that bustling, dirty, busy, noisy city, we toured Yves Saint Laurent's azur blue garden retreat.

It was refreshing. At the end of our one day in Marrakech, I got to indulge in a traditional spa at Hamman de la Rose, just on the edge of the medina near our riad.

It was a welcome unwinding and soothing to the soul to have a personal attendant scrub you down and bathe you like a baby. It washed away the dusty grime of the city, along with any residual suffering I was holding onto. It was a welcome hour of peace and solitude before heading out on the road the next day.

The morning came and we loaded up into jeeps — seven drivers with four or five passengers per car. It was the biggest group that Josef at Sahara Desert Camping Tours had ever seen!

Josef and his desert brethren had been taking folks into the desert near their hometown for years. He had trained his friends so they could start their own businesses. It was the first time he had such a large group that he could bring them all back together for this road trip — and what a road trip it was.

Rocking to music of Tinariwen, the famous Moroccan trance band — a mix of traditional Berber and Sufi rhythmic tunes — we rode FREEDOM across the country from Marrakesh east over the greater and lesser Atlas Mountains.

We stopped in Ouarzazarte, pronounced Wär'zazat — the Door to the Desert and Morocco's Hollywood where many famous movies were shot, from *Lawrence of Arabia* back in 1962 to more recent episodes of the *Game of Thrones*.

We ventured through the red sand Ait Benhaddou village built back in the 17th century, and sat atop the highest peak. Then onward to the desert to ride camels and sleep under the stars. We would experience much bonding and many moments of utter joy during this fantastic journey.

As we arrived in our drivers' hometown, I suddenly got a massive eye infection, not a condition conducive to sleeping in the desert. Josef stopped at the pharmacy to make sure I got some antibiotic ointment. Nothing was going to stop me from joining the caravan of camels heading deep into the dunes.

Wrapped in my traditional African desert cover and donning my shades, I was bound and determined to make this happen.

Camels are so cool. Our convoy cast classic long shadows over the dunes as the sun set over an undulating golden landscape. Arriving at the desert camp just as the light faded, we gathered for a traditional dinner of tagine — a dish we would quickly grow tired of.

As the drivers were winding up their after-dinner entertainment, I couldn't ignore the discomfort of, and lack of sanitation for, my eye infection. So I sought the clean safe haven of the hotel where we had left our luggage. Thankfully there was one man who could take me there.

Driving a four-wheel jeep across the high dunes in the dark is a very bizarre experience. You can't really see where you are going or which way the dunes are dipping until you are on top of them. This guy was my hero. Needless to say there was much laughter involved.

I can't say I was disappointed to sleep in a proper bed with clean sheets and no sand in my eyes, but I'll always wonder what it was like sleeping under the stars in the desert. That's a good reason to go back again one day.

The next day, after all the sand was washed off, we piled back into the jeeps to continue our adventure. Next step – Fez, quite possibility one of the most fascinating places I've seen.

HIRE A GUIDE

Fez is the second largest city and the cultural and spiritual centre of Morocco. Over one million people call it home, many of whom live in the UNESCO heritage site of the Fes el Bali Medina. This medieval town dates back to the 800s, and its complex maze of over 12,000 lanes, alleyways and dead-end streets is mesmerizing. These 'streets' are only wide enough for pedestrians with their carts and mules, of course.

The medina is huge! Each of its subsections is defined by a mosque (place of worship), a hammam (bath house), a communal bread oven, a fountain and madrasa (school). Fez boasts the oldest university in the world.

I didn't even know this place existed until we were looking for a place to stay for the night before heading back to Rabat. In hindsight, Fez is well worth a longer visit, so it will be staying on my bucket list for further investigation.

MAZE OF CONFUSION

It was late and dark when we arrived. There were too many of us to fit in one riad, so the group was divided in two. Each group was escorted separately deep into different parts of the medina, where we made so many lefts and rights that my brain lost track, and my breadcrumbs ran out.

Consumed by the darkness like some intoxicating quicksand, we finally arrived at our riad guesthouse, Riad Saada. Another incredibly beautiful three-story palace, its rooftop afforded views that stretched as far as the eye could see. The medina lights were aglow — it was a magical site.

The high cement walls interrupted the internet signal inside the medina, creating a communications breakdown between the folks in the two separate riads. After settling in, our host left us to fend for ourselves. Shortly after, we discovered that JP and Adrian from the other riad had decided to find their way over to our riad without a map, directions or access to internet. Epic fail.

The medina madness was upon them. They were lost for ages. Not a word. We were petrified. I could not imagine how they felt. Wandering around dark laneways and alleys without directions, they could have been robbed or worse, kidnapped

— even though JP is over six feet tall and built like a bear. It's amazing what your imagination will conjure up.

When we tried to step outside to look for them, we were pelted by stones thrown from the shadows. It was probably just a bunch of mischievous kids, but it sent us screaming like young children back inside, not to emerge again until our guide showed up at the designated time next morning.

I never did find out what happened to JP and Adrian that night, but they eventually made it back to their own riad safe and sound. In a smaller group, we were off to experience the medina madness in the daylight with an official guide this time — the *only* way to go.

THE FASCINATING HISTORY OF FES

We learned a lot about the history, the culture and the Islamic traditions inside the medina. We wandered through the souks (smaller markets inside the medina) each with its specific services or wares — the tailor, the kitchen supply guy, the butcher, the baker, the candlestick maker.

The Fez el Bali medina is also home to the famous Chouwara tannery, a smelly, colourful tourist trap where guides are sure to make a few extra Dirham for taking their followers on a tour. After receiving mint leaves at the front door to mask the stench, we discovered a myriad of leather products over several floors.

I really wanted an authentic tan-coloured pouffe — the traditional embossed leather ottoman — and for some reason I was determined to buy it there.

After my usual laborious selection process, I finally bought one but later found out that I paid way too much — then bought four more as gifts for the same price back in Rabat.

That overpriced pouffe was worth every penny as it sits in my bedroom and reminds me every day about my experience in Fez and the Desert Adventure.

TRAIN BACK TO REALITY

Our train ride back to Rabat later that day was a chance to digest the events of the past few days. I was so full of experiences and ready to get back to a normal routine, whatever that means in this whirling, swirling life of a digital nomad. Just something that remotely resembled normal would be great. Besides I had a lot of work to catch up on — business was ramping up.

THE VADER DEATH CALL

I was quite proud of my emotional resilience as I bounced back from the various setbacks during that trip. But then came EID – the 3-day Festival of Sacrifice marking the end of Ramadan, when families and friends gather to feast and feed those less fortunate. One of the most famous traditions of this festival is the sacrifice.

The butcher has a busy schedule that day, with back-to-back killings throughout the city. The blessed animals are kept in backyards, courtyards or any space available, for days until their numbers are up. For an entire week after my return from the desert, I listened to these sheep bleating their echoing Darth Vader cries for help all day and all night. Until the rear sanctuary of our apartment block became an abattoir.

Then silence. Thank Allah, I did not have to witness the sacrifice. But from my balcony I could see the grim display of the celebrating chefs cooking their kill over open pits in the gutter. Blackened parts were strewn as children played, while the sun set on another day in Rabat.

As if the tile in the kitchen wasn't bad enough, the sacrificial scraps pushed me to the edge of my HAPPINESS once again. I needed to get out of Rabat.

CHEFCHAOUEN

I couldn't wait to trade one chef for another, Chefchaouen — the Blue City — a city like no other I've ever seen. Entirely painted in blue, this is a peaceful, yet powerful place just south of Tangier in the north of Morocco.

Nestled in the cleavage of the Rif Mountains, its endless blue buildings adhere to the hillsides as if cradled in its breasts. The origins of the blue came with European refugees from the past, who believed that if they painted their homes the color of the sky they would be closer to God. It was a five-hour drive for a weekend of transcending bliss.

When I woke up on Saturday, the light streamed in the tiny window peeking at me from my combo bathroom/shower room hidden behind the Moorish-shaped doorway. Outside my bedroom on the third floor of this blue medina home, was a balcony that revealed another world, another way of life.

White linens on the line gently billowed in the light breeze — a new day on earth, a new place to stay, and a new way to play on this remote journey. Our rooftop terrace was an awe-inspiring perch where the ritual call-to-prayer vibrated through the soul. That evening as the sun dipped slowly behind the mountain, I stood inhaling this wondrous moment with my friends, Dan, Jen, Renee and Sue — a memory we will always cherish, a moment that will be embedded in my soul forever.

HIMOU

Himou works in a little shop next door to our Airbnb. He is a Berber, the aboriginal people of Morocco. He makes Chefchauoen (or Chauoen, for locals) his home for the summer to sell blankets, rugs and clothing made by his black Berber tribe.

His real home is deep in the desert, where he is one of the many patriarchs of a nomadic group of 25 families. They live in tents, as one with each other and with nature, practicing the traditional rituals of generations that have gone before them.

Once travelling freely throughout the country, the Berbers escaped into the mountains and Sahara desert when the Arabs forced a conversion to Islamic beliefs. Most Berbers converted but some still remain true to their tribal traditions and naturalistic rituals.

Over tea in the back of the little shop where he stores the fruits of his people's labour, Himou told me tales of the tribe. Like many earth-based religions, they take lessons and find the connection to God in nature.

The Berbers live their lives by the four directions:

- In the north, they find Peace in their minds.
- In the south, they walk with Love in their steps.
- In the west, they spread the abundance of positive Energy.
- In the east, they find the Light that eliminates the darkness.

He showed me a navigation amulet that is used when the tribe moves locations. A small hole in the top acts as a viewfinder to read the stars and show the way at night. His tale was so enchanting, I bought the story — and the amulet. Which my son, Julian, now proudly owns.

He told us of the trance music they play to bring them closer to spirit – like our Tinariwen road rhythms. Himou told me there are different rhythms that reflect the vibrations of each of the bright naturally-died colors that adorn his tribe's artistry.

Their music induces an altered state from which they connect to spirits beyond the physical world. He played for me and I was entranced. I wonder what it would be like to live in the desert and commune with God in this way.

Himou himself is the healer of the tribe. He brings medicines from the city to cure illness or ease pain. He performs energy healing to clear the body, mind and spirit through the seven doorways of energy in the body. These seven doorways reside in the forehead, the shoulders, the hands and the knees. Much like chakras (from tantric tradition), these doors are the portals where energy can be given or received.

He demonstrated a clearing, and I felt the energy of his hands shifting my awareness. For many, a trip to Chaouen is an opportunity to take pictures of the endless blue walls, stairways, paths and doors throughout the medina.

Perhaps they stop to buy a few trinkets or ship home some carpets, blankets or leather goods. Few stop long enough to appreciate the true beauty of this city — the people who make it their home.

Himou is one of those people. He eagerly shares his culture. A culture that is alive and well but hidden from sight. If you find yourself in Chefchaouen, pay Himou a visit at the Akchour Bazar Galeria on Avenue Hassan 1, just west of the Ras el Maa (the river where locals gather to wash clothing and carpets.) Let him entrance you with his stories and music.

You may even find something you would like to take home to remind you of that time you had mint tea with him in his shop.

CASCADE COURAGE

When you make the journey to Chefchaouen, it's essential to visit the Cascades — the giant waterfalls on the other side of the mountain behind the city. I understand there is a long hike over the mountains if you are up for that kind of activity — we drove the long way around. The end of the road takes you to the welcome centre in Akchour.

But first a typical Moroccan breakfast with an egg, cheese, olives and bread.

I was eager for this walk in nature before our five hour drive back to Rabat that evening. It was a treacherous hike to the Bridge of the Gods, walking on slippery stones that crossed the river and boulders that border the shores. It gave me time to reflect on the wild ride over the past two months.

The journey was long and hot. In the cadence of our hike it was tempting to follow the steps of the person in front, even though they were younger, fit and more agile. Seeing their surefootedness gave me false confidence and I soon discovered that I needed to go at my own pace. Another in our group chose to wait out the hike at one of the makeshift cafés that dotted the riverside.

It was at moments like this that the generation gap seemed huge, just like the steps between some of those rocks.

Spiritual Hack

There are no 'should' steps in life. The person in front of you may hop from rock to rock, with agile ease. But that doesn't mean that is your course. Be careful before taking that next step, as their legs may have been longer, more stable or more familiar with the path. Perhaps they were ready to take more (or less) of a risk than you.

The way you navigate the rocky road of life is solely dependent on your perspective, confidence and skill. Working with your own competencies is critical in avoiding a severe slip or fall. Rocks are very unforgiving. Choose your own steps wisely.

As a leader on the path, you are navigating for your followers. Keep in mind the level of competencies of your team. At times you may take the wrong way, it makes sense to step back and reassess the trail and/or the destination. It may also be beneficial to let others take over and lead the way for a while. A good leader is also a good follower. That's why it's important to surround yourself with strong and capable people, then trust them to show you the way. It's a great and humbling honor to share the path with other powerful people.

The Akchour River and Chefchaouen brought peace back into my heart, but my return to Rabat seemed to trigger my emotional slide down the spectrum again. Simple day-to-day things were made more difficult. When my credit card was compromised, I instantly blamed Rabat. It was an easy target. But there is good and bad everywhere. As in most places in the world, Moroccans can be sweet and loving, ruthless and cunning all at the same time.

It wasn't long before I was feeling the tension of the city, relaxed on occasion by a Thai massage or the daily feast at the 7AY workspace. My goal was to overcome the intimidation

— to own this town and embrace the discomfort of the unknown. Charting the neighbourhoods, braving the old town medina and negotiating the post office so I could send a little piece of this magical, mystical place home along with some birthday gifts for the family.

As this five-week month slowly came to a close, I actually started to appreciate Rabat more and more. I had time to go back to Chaouen again — to take another dose of blue blissfulness. I was satiated, satisfied that I had taken the biggest drink of Morocco's secret sauce that I could handle. I will go back for more of that colourful chaos one day.

Month 3: Creativity and the Count

Destination: South Africa – Johannesburg; Bulgaria – Sofia; Romania – Transylvania ~ October

The purple blooms of springtime's jacaranda trees in the southern hemisphere make work feel like play. Then autumn in a northern post-communist bloc country can sure turn those blue skies to grey. But throw in a party at Dracula's castle and you won't really care what comes your way. HAPPINESS is a Halloween night to remember.

SOUTH AFRICA

It was time for our group to leave Morocco and fly to Eastern Europe, and the next city on our itinerary was Sofia, Bulgaria. But I had different plans. I had a 14,000 km detour ahead of me — flying across to Cairo and south to Johannesburg, South Africa.

Something about South Africa — the cradle of humanity — makes me feel at home. Maybe it's the drums, maybe it's the rawness of nature or maybe it's simply a calling.

I was invited to speak for my second year at ACRE – the 22nd International Creativity Conference in South Africa. ACRE is organized on an annual basis by the South African Creativity Foundation and is one of the most prestigious of its kind in the world.

ACRE is one of several creativity and innovation conferences I've been part of over the past 15 years. They were all born from the Creative Problem Solving Institute founded over 60 years ago by Alex Osborn (the originator of the term 'brainstorming' — think Mad Men) and the teachings of Sidney J. Parnes (a thought-leading educator at the time.)

Kobus Neething, the founder of ACRE, has been committed to bringing creativity to South African businesses for over 20 years, and included the educator-focused conference more than 10 years ago. The facilitators, trainers, consultants and coaches from around the world who speak every year at these conferences have become my family. It was a welcome dose of generational camaraderie.

These conferences allow me to do rewarding work, pushing the edges of people's thinking while pushing my own edges as a presenter.

Creative thinking and innovation invite us all to be change-makers in our lives, our communities and our organizations. It takes COURAGE to push beyond the status quo. That's what these conferences are about — personal leadership.

We teach people the skills to think differently, giving them the confidence to stand in their power and develop sound, creative ideas to make a better future. Personal leadership means we consciously co-create a new reality every day with our thoughts, words and actions — they all hold energy. So be careful what you think or say, you may be attracting exactly what you are asking for.

Mental Hack

Understanding the process of creative problem solving and learning the tools gives you the FREEDOM to co-

create more intentionally. You can learn more about it at conferences like ACRE, CPSI in Buffalo, NY or MindCamp outside Toronto, but here's a simple explanation of a fairly complex theory that breaks the creative problem solving process into four parts:

Clarifying — *Look at what is currently happening or assumed to be real. Gather all the information needed to determine what the actual problem is. So often people are focused on solving the wrong problem. Make sure the problem requires imagination to solve, needs an immediate solution, and there is someone with authority to solve it. Then set some criteria for success.*

Idea Generation — *Now it's time to get creative. This is what people typically call brainstorming. In fact, brainstorming is only one of hundreds of techniques to generate ideas — and lots of them. The more and wilder the ideas the better. Keep generating ideas even if you think you are finished. The best ideas come at the end. More minds make for more ideas — put two (or more) heads together to get better ideas.*

Development — *Take all the ideas and cluster, or categorize, them. Then consider which you will develop further — not just your favorites or the first idea you thought of. Here you work to strengthen your ideas and validate their positives, potentials and pitfalls (and how you'll overcome that challenge), building on the best to establish how you will move forward.*

Implementation — *Just as it sounds — this is where things actually get done, where the problem gets solved and you look like a hero. But remember, it's the setbacks that are the test of true COURAGE.*

The courage it takes to step up and lead this process is driven by your determination to make things right. Your personal power is limitless. You just need to have the right tools and to take a stand – like Nelson Mandela.

EXPANDING BORDERS

Each time I go to this conference at the Klein Karibe resort nestled in the wilderness outside of Bela Bela, about 1.5 hours north of Johannesburg, I venture further and further afield. The first year, I gathered the courage to take on Cape Town all by myself. The following year the conference brought me to Namibia and added Swaziland to the itinerary.

For me, life is an expanding opportunity to experience even more FREEDOM. It's important for me to stretch a little further afield each time, expanding out into the world, then contracting back into myself to learn the lessons as I go. It's starting to occur to me that I will probably expand so much this year that I may burst.

SMALL AND SOULFUL WORLD

Friday, October 14th is my birthday, and the last day of the conference this year. It was an incredible gift to have 250 people sing 'Happy Birthday' to me. What a lovely way to end the conference and start my birthday weekend with my family!

This annual pilgrimage gives me a chance to visit my cousin and his young family. Family is very important to me. As a first generation Canadian, I grew up with just my immediate family — mother, father, sister and brother — and I always longed to have deeper connections to my extended family. So I am grateful for the special treat of spending an extra week with them.

On Saturday night we attended a cool art market on the top floor of the parking lot at a shopping mall. It was refreshing to sip a cocktail and wander around admiring the beautiful arts and crafts. Then serendipity struck. As I stood pondering how I would get a gorgeous giant wall basket back to Canada, I started chatting with Heather, the young woman attending the stall.

It turned out that not only was she also from Canada, but she lives in my neighbourhood! As if that wasn't enough of a coincidence, she was also a best friend of Maudi, another one of my cousin's daughter from Holland, both of whom had made Swaziland their second home.

I couldn't miss the opportunity to send Maudi a selfie with her bestie, Heather, at our small world encounter on the rooftop of the Hyde Park Corner mall in Sandton.

DANGEROUS CORNERS

Anyone who has been to Johannesburg knows that crimes of opportunity are high. 'Smash-n-grabs' are commonplace, so savvy drivers simply run red lights so as not to fall victim to this roadside crime. Most people live in gated communities or gated estates with a guard, or lots of security cameras. Unfortunately, it can be an unsettling place at times.

There are parts of Johannesburg you simply do not go to because of the high crime rate. They are called the NO-GO zones, and what used to be one of the most dangerous of these is now an up-and-coming neighbourhood in the Maboneng Precinct. It's home to the Arts on Main every Sunday. Inside is the funky open-stall prepared food Market on Main, where you can find anything from Rasta 'Vegetarian Love' stew to artisan chocolate to lollipops and liquor.

The blocks surrounding the main building are alive with artists, musicians and performers, all working hard to entertain a few coins from your pocket. The food is a feast; art is a feast for the eyes. The music and dance quench the thirsty soul. Like many parts of Africa, the vibrancy and reality of life is powerful and moving. This weekend was the perfect way to end my time in Africa.

It was just a short work-cation, but I know I will be called again next year. The 14-hour flight to Sofia gave me lots of time to digest my South African soul food.

BULGARIA — GETTING IT ALL IN!

Living for one month in each city is intense. Keeping on top of client work while settling into a new location every time had its challenges.

I developed my own general rules for arrival in each new city, the first being to get my SIM card as soon as possible. That way I could spend the first week getting my bearings — scout out the grocery stores, cafés and other supplies, find the fastest route to the co-working space and, of course, find my way home.

After that I would review the monthly RY activities and scout out other points of interest. The middle two weeks would be jammed with events juggled with business obligations (I had a lot of catching up to do this month.) By the last week, I would just be getting comfortable, and then it was time to leave.

WASTE NO TIME

Whether it was a four or five-week month, the process was the same. By the time I got to Sofia on October 18, I had only three weeks to make this all happen before our transition to Croatia at the beginning of November. The transitions always took place on a weekend, so that it would be less disruptive to those working 9am-5pm, or 4pm-midnight Eastern European time.

Luckily, in my business I have flexibility to work any time of the day. I often worked in the mornings, which made me look like a hero when my clients woke up on the other side of the ocean to see their finished projects in their inboxes! I also like to work late at night, so was available for meetings later in the day in EST.

Work Hack

When planning your remote working itinerary, be sure to consider the time difference at your destinations and how it will affect your ability to connect with work back home.

Think about what you are willing to compromise in sleep patterns and lifestyle to work remotely. Then discuss it with your clients, teams or boss to see if there may be some accommodations for time zones.

Be mindful that although they may say, "No problem", in the unpredictable world of business you may still have to be part of those meetings at 3 am Asia time.

BONDING OVER BANITSA

When I arrived in Sofia, the rest of the Remotes had already settled in, bonding over Balkan *banitsa* (traditional Bulgarian pastry) and beer. Many lived together in the same apartments or buildings nearby, creating more tight-knit friendships and kindling romances.

It was wonderful to see how their relationships had grown, but I was feeling disconnected. Having been away from the group for over two weeks added to my sense of separation, and reconnecting with peers in South Africa had emphasized the differences between me and my Ikigais and 'gals.

I'll explain why in the next chapter, but I was allocated a one-bedroom apartment quite far from the co-working place. Being far away from everything didn't help my sense of separation, although I must say it was probably the most comfortable bed I had all year.

A STITCH IN TIME

I arrived from South Africa on a Tuesday and was eager to reconnect with people. Some of the Ikigals were gathering for a good 'ol "Stitch and Bitch" that evening. (In case you don't know, that's a Hen Party with needles and yarn.) Apparently there's a resurgence of knitting in subcultures, with groups gathering at local libraries, cafés and yarn shops to chat, learn and knit. Who knew?

What made this evening even more special was the invitation to support a local refugee camp in Bulgaria, where volunteers were teaching refugees to knit as a therapeutic pastime.

Lucille, Lucy or the "Loose Seal" as she was affectionately called, led the charge. Her personal goal was to knit a scarf with a bit of yarn from each of the countries we visited — back in Chefchauen I helped her find the elusive Moroccan yarn shop to get her fix. She was also busy knitting everyone a pair of Ikigai socks. (Lucy, if you are reading this, I'm still waiting for mine!)

A small group of five gals — Orna, Michelle, Kristen, Lucy and I — met at the yarn store to get our supplies and buy extra for the refugees. After some of the gals stopped to buy food, we started across town to their apartment.

In my excitement to join the group and get back to knitting, something I used to do a lot, it occurred to me that I hadn't followed my own rules. I was about to wander off into the dark night, and as I had not yet bought a local SIM card I had no data to find my way home.

I had no idea where I was going or how to get back to my apartment. So rather than risk getting lost in a new city, I decided to follow the breadcrumbs home. I was sad to miss the bitch session, but happy I was able to help with the refugees.

LAUGH IT OFF

Whenever I start to feel a little low, it's time to pick myself up and go. I was thrilled that Mike had spotted a British comedian performing that Thursday evening at The Comedy Club. I was feeling hum-drum — nothing a little laughter couldn't overcome.

Stephen K. Amos was hilarious. His dry British humor lightened up the politically fueled, subversive humor of eastern European. It was refreshing to get a dose of his quirky perspectives on everyday life, relationships and popular culture. A good comedian can help you look at life from a completely different perspective. Sometimes that's all it takes to bring more HAPPINESS into your world.

Emotional Hack

They say laughter is the best medicine and it's true! Have you heard of Laughter Yoga? Seriously, this is a thing. Google it. There are even online courses at Udemy and a Laughter Online University where you can become a certified laughter practitioner.

Laughter is scientifically proven (even Nandita, our resident RY brain science expert, agrees) to fool yourself into feeling happy. I've been practicing this for years. It's just so simple — and it works!

If you're not convinced, just head to a local comedy club or watch a funny movie.

When you get laughing, life will be so much easier.

KEEP IT COMING

On Friday night a bunch of us attended the "*Fire of Anatolia — TROY*" performance at the National Palace of Culture. It was a great show and I was happy to be back with my 'gais. What a wonderful week to arrive with events in full swing!

Saturday was a daylong yoga retreat hosted by our gracious and lovely local Experience Lead, Laura Slavov, at her family's beautifully converted country house. Now called the Bakyovo Retreat Center, it's about an hour-and-a-half outside the city.

It was beautiful — the perfect day to stretch my body and come back into myself.

Yoga practice is a wonderful way to be mindful of what is going on inside, as the quiet movements with closed eyes force you to focus internally. It gives space for your mind to SCREAM for attention, and I became increasingly aware that my sense of separation was simply a product of my own mind.

Like most human beings, I create stories to confirm the recurring fears that feed my feelings. My major fear is the fear of rejection. As I lay on the floor, I watched my tangled thoughts weave a nasty web of FEAR - False Evidence Appearing Real.

As I attempted to pull myself into the pigeon pose, I released those self-worth-sucking notions out of my mind. Breathing out the judgment of self and others, then breathing in the intention of open-minded, open-hearted, unconditional love. At many times over the year, this would be my practice, to keep me sane and centered.

Spiritual Hack

Don't lay blame or pass judgment. The simple practice of discernment and living by your own values far outweighs making choices based on what's important to others. When you live by other people's agendas, you will never know the FREEDOM of your own soul. You be you.

Practicing discernment with loving kindness is easy when you are lying on a mat in the middle of a gorgeous valley, surrounded by the autumn colours. It's much harder when you are triggered by others and situations out of your control. That's why they call it a practice. Nobody should expect perfection — just practicing mindful and committed thoughts, feelings and actions.

When you fill yourself with love there is no room for pain.

MOUNTAINS OF FUN

When it was time to get away from work, I would head to an RY event, wander through the city or join others on day trips into nature. The beauty of Bulgaria is in the great outdoors.

This eastern European country, just north of Greece, is full of mountains. Its eastern border meets the Black Sea north of Turkey.

Earlier in the month, most of the Remotes had discovered, and highly recommended, a day hike up to the Seven Rila Lakes. These are the most visited glacial lakes in all of Bulgaria, and when you get up to between 2100 and 2500 meters above sea level, you can certainly see why.

The first part of the ascent can be done by ski lift or off-road jeep — after my driving stories, I'm sure you know exactly which option we took! Little did Samvita and Laura, my hiking pals, know they would be laughing uncontrollably the whole way up.

As we bounced and jounced up the mountain runoff, ricocheting off rocks, pebbles and dirt slides, my giggles got gigglier. By the time we reached the meadow to start our hike we were all smiling with delight.

My intoxicating laughter was quickly thwarted by the challenge that lay in front of me. What I didn't realize was how much this trek would test my COURAGE.

The hike to the top of the mountain takes several hours, revealing new lakes the higher you go until you can see all seven lakes from the top. The incline starts slowly for the first hour, but then ascends quite rapidly — all with minimal oxygen available to breath at this high altitude.

My default position is sitting in front of my computer. They say sitting is the new smoking, and at the time I did both. So now I was going from dormant to dynamic on minute rations of oxygen! My heart was pounding out of my chest, but thankfully I've been blessed with a strong and resilient body, and a defiant will to keep me going.

Up, up, up we went — passing The Lower lake, The Fish lake, The Trefoil and The Twin lakes. We had to take a stop-action jumping shot in front of The Kidney Lake. Then on we went to The Eye Lake and finally the Tear. They call it the Tear because of the shape, but my theory is that it's because by the time you see it you'll be in tears.

The last ascent to the top of the highest mountain in the Balkans takes you up a slippery shale slope. In the summer it's a hot, dry climb, but in the winter it's most treacherous with snow and ice. October is the shoulder season, so it could go either way. On this day there were remnants of melting ice from a previous snowstorm.

As we stared up at this ominous cliff, a little inner voice spoke, "You don't have to do it if you don't feel safe." It wasn't a fearful or frightened voice. It was a very sensible, logical and caring voice that simply gave me the COURAGE to say 'no'. So I gracefully agreed, and stayed at lake number six while the others finished the final ascent of the mountain above.

Some may say I copped out. I'm a quitter. I'm lazy. I disagree.

Social pressure is great when you are ready to take a big leap in life, but there are times when just enough is just perfect.

I've always felt compelled to keep up with the group or stay the course or keep to the plan, but today I drew the line. I was proud of what I had already achieved on the climb, and I was satisfied. There was no need for me to push any further. There was a huge lesson in that for me: sometimes it takes COURAGE to quit when it feels right. And I was amazed at the feeling of FREEDOM I had from making that decision.

Our guide, Kiril of AzimutTours.com, was wonderful. He validated my concern that the climb might leave me overtaxed and the steep descent would surely send my knees into a raging protest.

Timing was important, as we needed to get back down in time to go to the Kotvata Sapareva Banya spa. No compromise there — this gal has her priorities straight! That sorely needed soak in the special baths was a lifesaver before the hour-and-a-half drive home.

Physical Hack

Go for the top, but stop before it becomes dangerous.

Peer pressure can often cloud our judgment, making us do things that might not be so smart. It's great to be part of the dynamics of a group, but have the confidence to say no if you need to.

A good guide should never push you beyond your abilities. Heed your own values when being put on the spot to do something out of your comfort zone. Take calculated risks and choose based on your own inner guidance. Then be at peace with your choices.

Remember the over-abundance of COURAGE is recklessness.

I'm glad I made the choice not to finish the climb. The six lakes left me a little bent but not broken, so the next days were quite comfortable as I returned to life in front of a computer.

SPIDEY SENSE

The few short weeks in Bulgaria built up to a big, big, big event. (Did I say it was big?) Aaron, one of our intrepid side trip organizers, had organized an unprecedented trip to Transylvania to celebrate Halloween in Dracula's castle — an un-freaking-believable adventure!

Not many folks have **that** on their bucket lists — never mind having it checked off! It was an incredible opportunity to dial up the FREEDOM factor, be playful and act like a kid again.

I needed a costume! How does one do that in a foreign country? Call a friend — you know, the one who has worn pretty much every costume in the book. For me, that was fancy dancin' Nancy, fondly named after our two years of belly dancing together. She is an inspiration in many ways, and of course she had the perfect solution.

I spent the next few days looking around Sofia for supplies. All I needed was three pairs of black tights, large safety pins, some stuffing and some string. Assembly was simple. Cut off the panty parts of the tights, leaving only the legs. Stuff the legs with whatever soft stuffy stuff you can find, leaving space for little joints where they can bend and be tied. Tie the strings between the legs so they look like spider legs. Then safety-pin the stuffed spidery legs strategically to whatever you're wearing — which must be black, of course. Tie the ends of the strings to your wrists so that you can move your spidery legs around like a marionette. Voila — you're a spider!

TRANSYLVANIA EXPRESS BUS

The morning finally arrived. The 8am meet-up at the bus came early, but there was lots of time to settle in during the 12-hour ride. Drinkers in the back of the bus, please! With all the stops to replenish drinks and the endless line-ups in the one-bathroom gas stations along the way, it turned into a 16-hour drive from Sofia to Rasnov, Romania.

The driver was not a happy camper. The last few hours were in the pitch dark on hairpin turns up and down the side of a mountain. At times like this the front row seat can be a blessing and a curse, and Rasnov could not come soon enough for the swaying soldiers on that bus.

It was a modest little town. We rolled up to different stops and poured into our beds for the night. Thank goodness for Airbnb – how else would you possibly find rooms for 35 people in a tiny little place like Rasnov?

After breakfast, a bunch of us set off to Brasov, taking the cable car up to the lookout and wandering the square before heading back to prepare our personas for the Hallow's Eve.

As night came we made our way to the castle. Our entrance ticket to the party included a tour of the castle first — a frightfully fascinating place! Its hallowed halls and secret staircases made it intriguing to imagine how the infamous Dracula spent his days — and his nights.

Creepy characters of all descriptions emerged in full regalia that night. There were the typical ghosts and goblins, glittery witches and scary skeletons, the living dead — and too many Draculas to *count*.

The party was held in a giant tent on the front lawn under the mysterious musical projections on the castle above. The leaf-bare trees of autumn cast eerie shadows on the ground. The music thumped as dark, shadowy figures contorted to beats on the dance floor.

Our group stayed together, taking over a corner of the tent for the night. That allowed me to dance around the whole tent, weaving my spidery web in and out and around my "prey", oblivious to my sinister plan. Well I had to entertain myself somehow, because I couldn't hear a word anyone said! It was a fun way to pass the time. The party went on into the wee hours of the morning.

I don't really remember how we got home. All I know is that spending the night partying at Dracula's castle made me feel young and old all the same time. A beautiful balance of pure HAPPINESS!

Next morning we all met at the assigned location for the long trip back to Sofia. There, in the lobby of an unsuspecting hotel, a crumpled mess of post-party casualties piled in a heap, we waited — and waited — and waited.

An hour past our scheduled departure there was still no bus. We were convinced that the driver was so pissed off about our shenanigans on the way to Romania, that he couldn't stand the thought of having us all back in his bus for another 16 hours.

We waited some more. Some bailed, renting cars or taking Ubers to airports. The rest of us sat in shock, sure we were stranded. Oh ye of little faith!

When you are on a journey so great with so many obstacles, it's important to know you're in for the long haul. Yes, there is always an Uber to save you, but if you hang in there for just a little longer, your bus will come too.

When the bus finally arrived, it was a much quieter ride back to Bulgaria that day. As we drove up around the hairpin turns of the Carpathian Mountains, daylight revealed the jaw-dropping landscapes we had negotiated in darkness the night before. Gulp!

The Romanian countryside is lovely. In fact, it's hard to believe this beautiful place is best known for its famous vampire, Dracula – the fictitious character created by Bram Stoker. The Count Dracula character was loosely based on Vlad Dracula or Vlad the Impaler, who ruled this region from 1431-1476. Not a very nice guy from what I understand.

COUNT DOWN TO TRANSITION DAY

The history just kept coming during my last week in Sofia. Between designing and publishing my client's book, doing endless design revisions for another client, working on my own video elearning series and sorting out utility bills from home that had gone astray, I managed to do the Communist City Tour and visit the Rila Monastery, the largest and most famous Eastern Orthodox monastery in Bulgaria. We got a real taste of just how strict that Orthodox rules are when we got kicked out for talking in the church. Yikes — bad tourists!

This group is not one to abide by strict rules of covenant. We are rule breakers and trendsetters. We are Ikigai.

Month 4: Road Trips and Romance

Destination: Croatia – Split, Dubrovnich, Zagreb; Italy – Ancona, Tuscany, Venice ~ November

The tourists are gone. Most of the beach restaurants are shut down for the season. We are flirting with winter but not committed yet. Most days are lovely but the chilly ocean breeze can blow in an eerie fog without warning. Cold weather warms the heart. Feel the FREEDOM to fall in love. Go deep but prepare yourself – Winter is Coming

Flying in and out of Split during the off-season is a challenge, especially with a large group. However, nothing is too much of a challenge for the RY travel team, who arranged for a VIP experience. Our luggage would travel separately so we could fly on a private jet from Sofia to Split – very posh.

I'll never forget arriving at the Split airport and deplaning on the tarmac into a shuttle bus. The bus drove less than 100 feet/30 metres and we were directed to get off and enter the terminal. Seriously! Why didn't they just let us walk?

Maybe it was part of the VIP service.

Traveling with a concierge may seem indulgent, but it's worth every penny if you are working while traveling. Some things are just not worth agonizing over, especially for me with my propensity for exhaustive searches before making a purchase decision.

I can spend hours, days, or even weeks staying up into the wee hours looking for and coordinating flights, accommodations and transfers to any destination. I can't imagine coordinating an entire year on my own. It would take me a year to plan it!

TRAVEL THREE TIMES

I have a theory that you actually travel three times —

1. Planning – Imagining what the destination will be like and picking the right place to stay in the right neighbourhood — close to transit, etc. Figuring out how you might spend your time, what your options are, what are the must-sees and how to make it all happen.

2. Being there — This is where you can reap the benefits of all that time you spent in researching, booking and anticipating your needs. It's the time to really enjoy the experience, although it will often be punctuated by more research and expanded itineraries.

3. Reliving it — The categorizing, backup and review of all the pictures, posting on social media or a blog,sharing stories, journaling about it (or in this case writing a book).

What seems like a pretty simple three-step process can be exhilarating and exhausting at the same time — it's exhilarausting! This Portmanteau (blended word) captures the essence of my entire year.

EVERY CULTURE HAS A DIFFERENT LANGUAGE

Another blessing of traveling with this group is that there are all ages, backgrounds and experience levels, and everyone brings a little something different to the table. It certainly came in handy with all the languages we had to navigate so far: Portuguese, Arabic and French in Morocco, Bulgarian, Romanian, Croatian — and that was only four months in.

Our fearless Colombian darling, Laura, or LG for short, offered a free Spanish class back in Lisbon, and then Brendon stepped up in Morocco to share his Arabic skills. We somehow managed to fake our way through Bulgarian and Romanian, thanks to English speaking locals.

In Split, Marco, our Croatian national Remote, gave us his version of the Croatian language. Not surprisingly it was very skewed to drinking, and the social culture of, you guessed it — drinking.

Croatians are unapologetic, not only about their drinking but pretty much everything. When Erica asked Marco, "How do you say 'I'm sorry' in Croatian?" he said, "We never say that." Nor do they say "thank you" for that matter. Don't even try the random smiling at people, which just makes them feel uncomfortable. It must be the residual effect of communism.

Tribal Hack

Look not for what you can get out of your travel community but how you can give. The first step in bonding is sharing your gifts, your experiences and your love.

EVERY PLACE IS HOME

About a month ahead of each new destination, we were able to update our accommodation preferences — shared or solo, close to workspace, kitchen, big bed, lots of light, etc. There was a list of options, but there were always trade offs — you can't have it all.

It was Claire's unenviable task to match up everyone's preferences with the available accommodation in each city. I was always happy with my apartments and my roomies when I had them — except for Morocco, of course, where I loved the roomie and hated the apartment. But I always preferred to have my own place, with the option to work from home and not be in anyone's way. That's how I ended up in that apartment far away from it all in Bulgaria.

I loved my sassy little apartment in Split. It was awesome. Although I didn't have the view others had of the ocean over WIP, the co-working space, I had my own little garden, and the interior was beautiful — brand new modern décor, nice kitchen, two lovely bathrooms and two bedrooms. The other bedroom was for our favourite ghost remote, Svetlana, who would fly in on occasion just to say she was part of the program.

EARNING YOUR SUPERLATIVE

I believe it was in this apartment in Croatia that I came to earn my superlative. You know those titles people get in their high school yearbook, the ones that say, "Most Likely to ..."? Well the Ikigais had a yearbook too.

Svetlana wasn't scheduled to arrive for a couple of weeks, so I got to try out which bedroom I wanted for the month. Like Goldilocks, I slept in one bed, then I slept in the other. The first one was *way* too hard and the second one was *way* too hard. No, that's not a typo. I mean harder than hard — like a piece of wood with a little bit of cushion for looks.

I endured a week of painful sleepless nights until I built up the COURAGE to beg our local ops person if I could have a foam mattress topper. I was instructed to submit a "ticket" in order to have my request fulfilled, a request even I thought was *over-the-top*, but I just wasn't prepared to suck it up for an entire month.

My attitude is "If you don't ask you don't get." So I had to ask and — I got the most precious gift of a three-inch thick memory foam topper for my bed. I was so excited! I could actually sleep and not wake up aching all over. It was even more appreciated a week or so later when I fell ill with food poisoning and follow-up kidney infection.

I guess it was only natural that I was voted the Person-Most-Likely-to-Submit-a-Ticket in the RY Ikigai Yearbook — a nickname I was proud to own if it meant I could get a decent night's sleep.

HAPPINESS IS A NEW FACE

As I mentioned at the beginning, each Remote Year group travels with two leads. Claire was our Program Lead and Orna was our Experience Lead — until she wasn't. Orna was leaving the program and we were getting a fresh, new face. This new Experience Lead would travel with us for the rest of the year, so we were all excited to see who it was.

Meet Gianni, young and vibrant with lots of charm. His big, beautiful smile perfectly matched his bright, engaging eyes, and his infectious energy seriously boosted the fun factor. I saw something very special in Gianni, and over the next eight months he became my surrogate travel son.

Apparently, Remote Year found Gianni relaxing on a beach in Bali. Prior to that he had been leading high school students around Asia on summer programs. After dealing with teenagers, how hard would it be to entertain us? He made it seem effortless.

WORKING HARD OR HARDLY WORKING

They say variety is the spice of life, and Croatia offers lots of that — from the vast network of adjoining countries with deep and varied history, to the bold mountains in the interior and the rocky outcrops along the coastlines, to the sunny, sandy shores of Split. The latter is where our WIP co-working space was located.

This idyllic spot had picture window views of the beach and the ocean. The sunsets were spectacular, and the temptation to indulge in the seaside lounge life was palpable. The ultimate FREEDOM!

One of the joys of the digital nomadic life is the ability to work wherever there is wifi, while sipping a cocktail and watching glorious sunsets. The only problem is trying to stay focused on the work.

During our time in Croatia, Mike, the British brand guy, brought together a group of us to invest our time and talents in pitching business for his company. It was an interesting experiment to see how a group who played together could work together under the pressure of a pitch.

In the end, we didn't win but it was a great way to learn more about each other's work styles and talents. This also created more opportunities to build business relationships on the road.

Social Hack

Use a co-working space to work on the road. Relationships you build there may sustain your travel. It's all about being in the right place at the right time and continuing to build your network.

MY OFFER

During our first orientation day back in Lisbon, I had promised to host a retreat, so my gift to the group this month came in the form of the Find Your Ikigai Retreat. I'm not going to lie, it took a lot of COURAGE to put it out there and open myself up to possible rejection by the group. Maybe that's why it took me four months to do it, or maybe I just needed to find the perfect time and place to make it happen.

That perfect place was Suncokret Holistic Yoga Retreat Centre on Hvar Island, a healing island where lavender blows in the breeze and olive trees birth a bounty of deliciousness. The island retreats date back centuries, having been used by the Ancient Romans for rejuvenation and renewal.

I developed the *Find Your Ikigai Retreat* based on knowledge and materials I'd gathered after studying spiritual laws for over 18 years with my mentor, Tanis Helliwell, through the International Institute for Transformation.

Five brave souls joined me on the journey; Bri, Hilary B, Jen, Jordan and Lee. After a two-hour ferry ride on Friday evening, we landed in Stari Grad after dark, so we had no idea what awaited us. Our hosts, Evening (seriously, her real name) and her husband were great. They picked us up, tucked us into our respective rooms and made sure we were warm enough as the temperatures dropped.

The next morning we awoke to an incredible gift. Propped above the tiny little town of Dol Sveta Ana, their small country house was perched on the side of a mountain. Spread out in front of us was an expansive landscape of rolling hills that led down to the water, with horizon views of other Croatian Islands. It was indeed the perfect little piece of paradise to discover our Ikigai.

The idea of the retreat was to do just that — retreat from the noise and busyness of travel, sit quietly with our thoughts and invite nature to help us discover the soft, quiet voice within. I based the facilitation design on the five levels of needs and values model that I use with everything in life — physical, mental, emotional, social and spiritual.

As part of our spiritual self-discovery, I used a tool common to the North American aboriginal cultures and, as I had discovered earlier from Himou in Chefchauen, it is also part of the Moroccan Berber tradition. It's called the Four Directions.

These cultures believe that all we need to know is already inside us, and that we can access our higher knowing by calling in the spirit of nature. The Four Directions: North, South, East and West, each carry qualities that are aspects of our own lives. Tapping into these qualities and using them to answer questions provides clarity and purpose in our choices.

Spiritual Hack

To learn more about self-discovery and the Four Directions tool in my blog on NiceLife.ca

---

The group emerged relaxed and reflective, each with their own insights to move forward with their purpose. I still cherish the handwritten feedback they gave me about our few days together, and I still pray for each and every one of them to continue to follow their calling.

BRACE YOURSELF – WINTER IS COMING

We seem to be chasing winter. Croatia in November was certainly heading in that direction. Winter was starting to blow its chilly winds around every corner this month.

It seemed appropriate that we would also visit Dubrovnik, the walled city used as a location for filming the Game of Thrones. "Winter is Coming", the Stark House metaphor from Game of Thrones, suggests you must always be ready because anything could happen. It's a warning that darker times may come unexpectedly in your life. So be prepared with the right clothing.

Physical Hack

My most valuable piece of clothing is my full-length Columbia winter quilted down jacket with reflective lining. It's so lightweight and warm. Get yourself a lightweight insulated coat. It's so small and versatile. It packs down to less than a 6" cube. Use it as a pillow, a blanket or a back support when you're not wearing it as a coat.

Our weekend in Dubrovnik was fast and furious. In two days and one night we walked around the walled fortress and the old town. We lunched at Kamenice, a little seafood restaurant in one of the squares, where the mussels were piled high and the wine flowed. Then hopped on a boat for the harbor tour.

The next day we were up the cable car for an outstanding view of the city. The town, harbor and surrounding islands looked miniature down below. We also managed to squeeze in a meal at the popular traditional Croatian restaurant called Konoba Dubrava, a short walk from the top cable car station.

I would have loved to stay longer but it was time to get back on the bus to Split.

MY ROOMIE IS COMING

The "Winter is Coming" was captured metaphorically later that month with a visit to the Museum of Broken Relationships in Zagreb, the capital city of Croatia.

It was Lee who suggested the bus ride to Zagreb, as she was off to see her friends in London for the holidays. My yet-to-arrive roomie, Svetlana, was flying in through Zagreb and had to drive to Split because of the off-season lack of flights.

So I decided to join Svetlana and help her navigate back to our apartment — any excuse to discover more of our host country was not lost on me. I was able to work on the bus and grab time to check out the city while I was there.

It was almost by accident one day that we found the Museum of Broken Relationships — a creatively-curated, continuously-growing collection of items illustrating the stories of how love went bad. Each installation had a story — engaging, sometimes frightening and mostly delightful in their vulnerability and truth. There was everything from a broken guitar ("The music was gone") to a basketball jersey ("He was a player"); from disconnected, demented, damaged items to a simple license plate from the car that sank into the river along with someone's one true love.

I highly recommend a visit if you want to feel better about your previous break-ups. You can reach out to them on their website brokenships.com, if you have an interesting story to share or you can 'pin' your break-ups on their interactive home page map. Their main collections are in Zegrab and Los Angeles, but they are expanding and on the move. Devastatingly brilliant!

Social Hack

Maybe this is a good place to include some safety tips on dating abroad.

I hear that some people who travel use Tinder to meet locals and learn more about the city they are visiting — hey, if you hit it off then you may get a more intimate view of the city! It goes without saying, but I'll say it anyway: meeting strangers in public is the wisest move. Heading off with them alone in a car can lead to disaster. One guy went off with his Tinder date and was driven to a quiet street where he was robbed and abandoned.

So pay attention to your reptilian brain (not the other one, guys) — it's the part that warns you of pending danger. If it doesn't feel right, don't do it. Do double dates until you build familiarity and trust. No matter how good someone makes you feel, you can never be too safe.

I'm not a Tinder gal but I did have a few fantasy encounters!

During my last week in Croatia, I struggled with the decision to take yet **another** side-trip. But Italy was so close. I had never been there and wasn't sure when I would get the chance again. I was becoming addicted to the FREEDOM of living in Europe with everything so close. So I took a four-day, three-night road trip to Italy. It started on a midnight ferry leaving the Split harbour, and arriving in Ancona at 8 am.

ITALY

Arriving on the overnight ferry from Croatia that morning, I waited for my turn to meet the border guard. It was love at first sight! Our eyes met. Sigh. He asked for my passport with his sexy Italian accent. He looked inside, then peered back at me with those baby blues and said, "Hmmmm... Toooroooontooo." It was the first time I had thought of my birthplace as dreamy.

My heart was pounding under my well-slept-in-travel-clothes. As he walked away to check me out on his computer, I checked *him* out. **Wow!** I haven't felt this way in a while. My head swirled.

Within minutes I saw myself moving to Italy. We would snuggle in each other's arms, sharing stories in our broken Eng-Italiano while sipping fine wine and looking out over the hills of Tuscany. Cooking together, we would entertain our very fashionable yet down-to-earth friends. We would grow old together and play with our grandkids in the garden. Life would be wonderful.

He was making his way back to my car. Gasp! What would I say? What would I do? How would I ever live without him?

Holding my passport open at a stamp with Arabic writing, he peered over the top and said, "Where were you in September?" I was mute with nervous infatuation. I couldn't speak. I couldn't even think. I had no idea what he was talking about. I was caught in the bliss of his deep blue eyes. My heart thumped even louder.

What could I say that was smart, pretty, appealing? Nothing. "I don't know," was all I could muster. He smiled at me warmly. "Miss Tooorooontooo, where were you in September? Syria?"

"No, no, no," I said, the gravity of the situation finally dawning on me — it was, after all, 8 am after a rather sleepless night.

"Morocco," I replied. We laughed together, just as I imagined we would for the rest of our lives. Then he returned my passport and waved me on with a smile and a twinkle in his eye.

I was still floating on a cloud as I merged into rush hour traffic. From there I aimed for Tuscany — another one of my top bucket list destinations. My heart still throbbing for my blue-eyed border guard, I pulled into a roadside café for my morning coffee. I'm not talking about your typical North America highway gas pump and coffee shop. This place had a cozy, local vibe, with folks sitting around enjoying their coffee and talking.

Nobody was in a rush, and I'm pretty sure I was the only one asking for takeout. The lady behind the counter smirked at me, "Americano?" she quipped and the whole café broke into laughter. In my sleepless, infatuated daze, I said, "*Si por favor.*" As the words left my lips I realized I was mixing my Latin languages — thank God I was too tired to care. I had never had an Americano in my life — how ironic that I would have my first one in Italy.

As my Americano arrived and I stumbled through yet another currency exchange (my seventh in four months), I felt someone looking at me.

A man was standing beside me, taking great interest in my disruptive presence. I grabbed the sugar and politely turned to smile. OMG — another dreamy Italian man! Our eyes locked for a fleeting moment until he motioned for me to look back at my coffee. During our enchanted encounter, which seemed to last another lifetime, I managed to pour sugar over the counter **beside** my cup!

In shock and dismay, I grabbed my coffee and ran out the door. Obviously, I had already fallen in love with Italy.

That was the closest I got to anything remotely resembling a relationship all year. However, Tuscany stole my heart. It's everything I ever imagined and more. Gorgeous rolling countryside, lush campos with romantic farmhouses — and the food! So fresh and fueled with love, like the 1980s film, *Babett's Feast*. No wonder the men are dripping with sex appeal.

I couldn't get enough of Tuscany in just one night, so decided to stay for two very cold nights at the beautiful Fattoria Voltrona near San Gimignano.

The FREEDOM to change plans in an instant is one of the other joys of the digital nomad's life.

Stretched out on a chaise lounge on a beautifully manicured vacation farm, working from my laptop while looking out over Tuscany, was a dream come true. I'm sure I could have shot the sequel to *Under the Tuscan Sun*, that charming little ditty from the early 2000s. But as magical as those two days were, it was time to move on.

Venice was calling me, and I followed the call to the north. I was blessed to stay at a fabulous little boutique hotel called The Bloom BnB in the centre of the floating city, courtesy of Hotels.ca. I do recommend you take your winter wear if you end up in Italy in November. Brrrr — I sure could have used one of those hot Italian men to keep me warm.

Travel Hack

Book your accommodations through Hotels.com and you get one free night for every ten nights you book. It's a wonderful perk for frequent travelers.

If it hadn't been for the cold and my pending departure with the group, I could have stayed for the rest of my life in Italy. It was a long drive back to Split. Which gave me plenty of time to reminisce about my loves and bid them a fond farewell.

Croatia was a delight. It's nicely positioned just outside the Eurozone, so the cost of living is much lower than in other parts of Europe. It's an affordable and beautiful destination, and I would definitely go back.

Our departure was again on a private jet directly to Prague, as flying off-season with a group made it cheaper than transferring through Zagreb.

Month 5: It's Christmas, it Must be Prague

Destination: Czech Republic – Prague; Netherlands – Vlaardingen, Amsterdam ~ December

Find your roots in tradition. Those roots will ground you and give you the COURAGE to fly. True FREEDOM is not completely untethered, but takes off when your feet are firmly planted on the ground. Watch out for those cracks in the sidewalk though. They may slow you down just enough to spend valuable time with people that are most important to you.

Our transition to Prague captured the highest high of our year. You've heard of the 'Mile High' Club, I'm sure. Well it wasn't quite that high, but it certainly was up there.

Another private jet whisked us away from Split to 30,000 feet, where we celebrated Magic (Mark) and Sami's birthday with a special delivery high-flying birthday cake from Sami's Mom. HAPPINESS on high!

Then we made history with a sky-high Mannequin Challenge. For the uninitiated, it's pretty much what it sounds like — a group of people remain frozen in action while someone walks around filming them. Then the one-shot footage is put together with Rae Sremmurd's "Black Beatles" song and done, you've succeeded at the Mannequin Challenge. It was popular in November 2016 and we were right on trend. That's something I did not expect to be — it sure helps to hang with the cool kids!

HOME AWAY FROM HOME

The local teams seamlessly orchestrated our arrival in Prague, whisking us away in style to our waiting apartments. It always amazed me how they managed to receive 70+ people and distribute us effortlessly to our assigned homes. In Prague, mine was a wonderful one bedroom in a building shared by other Remotes Nandita and Ankur, Becca and Jacob, and Hilary B, and only a few blocks from K10, the co-working space.

K10 was a beautiful old mansion that used to be home to the Swedish Ambassador to Prague. Working there was a pleasure, partly due to the in-house chef cooking up fresh meals every day. Their passcard system allowed us to charge whatever we wanted from the kitchen and pay at the end of the month — which was a bit of a shock when it was time to leave!

Besides the local businesses at K10, there was a large expat business community. That's because Prague is the type of place where people come and never want to leave.

There's something about this city that made me feel comfortably at home. Maybe it was being there in December, with the traditional markets that stirred memories of bygone days. Christmas starts a little later in Europe — after December 1st. They don't try to milk the commercial side of Christmas by launching off American Thanksgiving and Black Friday deals.

Europe really invites you to relax into the season with more authentic heritage. The Christmas markets host a variety of vendors, with joyful clients sipping mulled wine around outdoor heaters. A little dusting of snow allows the holiday lights to give everything a magical glimmer. From the massive turn-of-the-century architecture to the homemade ornaments, it all contributes to the HAPPINESS you expect to feel over the holidays.

Travel Hack

If you want a Christmas getaway without getting away from Christmas altogether, Prague is an ideal destination.

CREATIVE CONGA LINE

On our first day in Prague we attended our city preview event at one of the local markets located in Prazka Trznice, where the farmers market hall still holds its own amongst a sea of buildings in various states of age and repair. Most vendors offer electronics, but artisans are emerging with fervor.

The MINT market is one of the halls inside this football field sized market area. It's a funky space showcasing some of the city's Bohemian fashion talent and hosting the Slow Food Youth Network and their signature experience, Disco Soup. Check out their video on YouTube.

Disco soup is such a cool concept. We joined a giant soup-making conga line, chopping and dancing to the music. It was an awesome way to start the day, although I didn't stick around to enjoy the soup because there was so much more of the city I wanted to see. The free walking tour at Charles Bridge started at 1pm. We had just enough time to get there.

I had a chance to visit the market again the following week to buy ingredients for a more traditional soup-making event. That visit was made even more interesting by Anna Grossmanova, the founder of the Youth Slow Food Movement and curious culinary historian who blogs about dishes she is preparing from an old Czech recipe book she found. A few days later we joined her at a historic home to prepare *Bramboračka*, the Czech people's beloved potato soup, and their traditional fruit-filled dumplings dusted with icing sugar, *Knedlíky tvarohové.* Comfort food at its finest!

HUMANS NEED TRADITION

Traditions truly are what hold us together. Experiencing the old European ways during the holidays made me reflect on what's really important. We were traveling around the world, dipping our toes into so many different cultures, it sometime felt as if we were addicts, just looking for the next culture fix. Oftentimes we were so numb to the change we didn't stop to appreciate what was right in front of us.

Comfort Hack

No matter how far away you travel, you can't escape from tradition. Traditions are part of what makes you who you are. Go ahead and fly as far away as you want, but if you want some emotional security find the places that honor your traditions and that align with your values.

Sometimes we just need the comfort and security of traditional things that are respected, honored and celebrated. Find solace in a place that feels familiar — heck, for some people it's the shopping mall that makes them feel as if they are back home! Do whatever you need to do to ground you so that you can build up the COURAGE for more adventure.

There are lots of ways to live like a tourist in any country — in fact, that's probably the easiest way to live. Most tourism caters to those who don't really want to be too far out of their comfort zone. But isn't that the whole point of traveling?

When you are anchored in some tradition, you can reach further out to discover more. It's the principle of contraction and expansion. In order to grow outward, we sometimes need to go inward to reflect on our past, our history and own where we came from.

THE GHOSTS OF WAR

Now that Gianni was onboard and we had a stellar local team in Prague, Remote Year introduced us to the idea of track events. Rather than having a whole bunch of random events people could go to during each month, they were now organized around three different track themes. This created a meaningful experience for participants as well as the track event leaders.

Although we were committed to one track each month, there were options to trade or pick up additional events if people couldn't make it for any reason. I loved that option and exercised it whenever I could. I fondly referred to myself as a '*Track Crasher*', as I could be seen bouncing around between tracks on a regular basis. The track I crashed most often in Prague was called Conflict and Resolution. Events were arranged around the turmoil of WWII.

While we were there, the movie *Anthropoid* had just been released and we had the opportunity to attend a private viewing. The movie depicts the assassination of Reinhard Heydrich, the "*Butcher of Prague*". This resulted in Hitler's retaliation against Lidice, a small village thought to be the birthplace of the suspected assassins, two young men who had left the country to serve in the British Air Force.

Hilter's suspicion was wrong, but Lidice was leveled anyway, the land completely reshaped to literally wipe it off the map. We met Marie Supikova, one of only 17 child survivors, whose account was personal and heart wrenching. I'd never felt the war as vividly as I did that day.

My parents were young teens living in The Netherlands during WWII, and their town was occupied by the Nazis. My Mom watched her best friend taken away, and my Dad was forced to walk for days to get food at a farm in the north. I never understood his obsession with war movies. Why would you want to relive such horror? I always felt a resistance to learn more about it. But visiting Lidice transported me back in time, leaving a visceral impression that touched me to the bone.

Emotional Hack

Don't be an onlooker. Visit places with an open heart. Have the COURAGE to feel the experience, not just look at it. Keep in mind that we are all human with simple needs, hopes and desires. When you strip everything away, like those that are persecuted by war, we are all the same. When you stop looking at how we are different and focus on how we are the same, it opens up your capacity for compassion and more love. Isn't that what we all want in the world?

BONEHEADED MOVE

Another must-see outside Prague is the UNESCO World Heritage Site of Kutna Hora and its neighbouring town Sedlec. Kutna Hora was settled in the mid-1100s and is home to the first monastery in Bohemia.

Many towns in Eastern Europe suffered from the ravages of wars and plagues causing the graveyards to quickly fill to capacity. In the late 1200s, the Abbott of Kutna Hora was sent to The Holy Land. He returned with some soil, which he spread over the grounds of the Seldec cemetery.

Once word got out, the aristocracy from all around Europe clambered to make this their final resting place. Add more wars, the Black Death and natural aging and by the 1500s there were an estimated 40,000 to 70,000 skeletons to be exhumed.

So what to do? Give the job to a blind man, because after all nobody wants to see that! This very patient and creative monk of the order took lemons and made lemonade.

With the help of another artisan who came along over 300 years later, he created the most fascinating, though somewhat macabre, display of bones in the ossuary of the newly built church. He stacked skulls, dangled digits and created clavicle chandeliers, all in the name of honoring the dead and making more room for whoever was dying to get into the blessed cemetery. Today the Sedlec Ossuary is one of the most visited attractions in the Czech Republic and has inspired the themes of many films. It's a bizarrely beautiful place.

Even more bizarre were the events that led up to my visit. Lee and I had planned to meet at the train station and ride like the locals. It took some COURAGE to find my way there and even more so to get there on time. Not being a morning person, this is always a bit of a challenge.

In my usual style I was a little tardy, so I was texting Lee while racing along the very uneven, pitted, cracked, heaved sidewalks (you already know where this is going) — I hit a hole and I rolled over on my foot. I didn't miss a beat and kept on going but not before I heard a 'Krick!'

It wasn't until after we had toured the church, the town and the monastery and sat down for lunch that I admitted that 'Krick!' might be a crack. I walked a total of 15,000 steps that day, and when I got home I was in agony. I decided that night I should really see a doctor. Luckily I was able to get in the next day at the Canadian Medical Centre (a comforting name for a

Canadian), where I embarrassingly had to admit to my 'text-ident'. Sure enough my foot was broken — it might have been just a hairline fracture but it was certainly an afro full of pain.

Travel Hack

*Okay, so this is the part where I tell you to make sure you have the right type of insurance. There are two basic choices, **travel insurance** or **international medical insurance**.*

*Before my Remote Year, I discovered there is a difference between **travel insurance** (the one-time purchase we usually buy when going on vacation) and the renewable type called **international medical insurance** (for expats who live abroad or people who travel for a year or more.)*

*My insurance broker, Alex Routh from Protexplan.com explains, "Don't be confused by the term **travel medical insurance**, it is just **travel insurance** and is an idiomatic American term you will find on the web. The underlying assumption with **travel insurance** is that if something serious happens and you make a claim, the company basically does everything in its power to get you back home, (where you presumably have home medical insurance) so the **travel insurance company** can stop paying!"*

*Some **travel insurance** requires you to be covered by your at-home medical insurance plan. If you are no longer covered by your home plan, then the **travel insurance** you bought is no longer valid.*

It's important to also consider the rules of your home country/province/state medical insurance regarding your extended stay outside the country. Depending on the length of your absence, you may not be able to keep your at-home medical insurance. For example, in Canada, if you are out of the country for six months or more, your provincial healthcare coverage stops, leaving you with only one option: **international medical insurance**, *which is sold annually.*

You don't want to pay insurance in two places, but you also don't want to be without coverage if there is a gap on return trips home.

There are countless variations in policy coverage and plans, but the fundamental difference is international **medical insurance covers** *all elective and urgent treatment, not only accidents and emergencies as is the case with* **travel insurance**.

As long as you are not claiming for a pre-existing condition, you can actually get full treatment while you are anywhere in the world. **International medical insurance** *even covers long term hospital stays if your claim involves a new illness, and it can be far less expensive.*

As a long-term traveler you need to educate yourself on the insurance options that are best for your situation and how the industry works.

Whether you suddenly find yourself being launched off the back of an ATV in the Greek Islands or a jetski in Colombia — or landing awkwardly after jumping off a cliff in Croatia or bridge in Columbia, there is one rule you need to follow when you travel: call your **travel or medical insurance company first**. *They need to know what's going on in order process your claim. All travel and international medical insurers provide 24-7 assistance in house or contract this service to outside companies like iSOS.*

Whatever insurance you buy, make sure you have the number on speed dial in case of a medical emergency or urgent treatment.

I can't believe in all the years I've been traveling I never knew about international medical insurance. But then again, this is the first time I've been gone for a year.

TIME FOR WOODEN SHOES

Like all good things, my visit to Prague had to come to an end. My foot healed up pretty quickly but I can still feel a little ache when I walk on uneven surfaces — like the cobblestone streets of Amsterdam, my next destination.

I was able to spend Christmas with my cousins and favourite aunt and uncle in The Netherlands. Talk about tradition! It was a week-and-a-half of utter indulgence with all my childhood favourites — chocolate letters, sproopwafels, droopies (black licorice), marzipan and almond paste delights, the signature ijse cookies from the Molendijk bakery in Vlaardingen, my family hometown.

Add to all that the endless family visits, with many cups of strong coffee and even more cookies. Even though I could feel my blood sugar riding a behemoth rollercoaster, I was in HAPPINESS heaven.

This was the only time I've been away from my immediate family for Christmas, but it was the next best thing. What a fabulous way to spend the holidays. I'm so grateful for traditions, especial during Christmas.

My Christmas cupcakes with the help of cousin May-Brit.

Month 6: Rain in Spain Turns to Ice

Destination: Spain – Valencia, Barcelona, Seville, Granada, Tariffa ~ January

Winter caught us in Spain — a country with no central heating or insulation to protect us from that unexpected extreme cold. Bundle up! This month was quite a ride, ending with the coolest gig ever and an important trip back home. This is the halfway point. If only a year had more months, months had more days, days had more hours and hours had more minutes.

Transition day happened on New Year's Eve. We arrived in Valencia (pronounced 'Balenthia' with a smile), the hometown of our fearless leader, Claire, just in time for the New Year's Eve celebrations.

There have been far too many New Year's Eve parties in my past, and in recent years I have eased into the habit of staying in, curled up on the couch under a cozy blanket with a good movie — calling a few close folks at midnight and then calling it a year.

There was no pressure to attend the group event, but I thought it was important to hang with my new peeps. Claire was so excited that we would get to experience their traditional New Year's celebrations, so I couldn't miss that.

First we gathered at La Malquerida, a traditional Valencian restaurant, to chow down on an assortment of tapas (which would be one of the mainstays of our diet in Spain), then on to the club next door to eat a bunch of grapes really fast. Seriously.

At the turn of the 19th century, vine growers started the custom of eating twelve grapes at midnight, one for each clang of the clock tower bells. They believed that doing so would ward off evil and promise a good harvest for the year to come. I love these crazy superstitions. This cultural tradition lives on today around the country and is broadcast from the main square, Plaza del Sol in Madrid.

This is how it works:

- Each patron is handed a little bag of grapes (Usually it's sticky with grape juice so you are already feeling a little awkward and uncertain about how this is all going to play out.)
- Everyone watches as the clock strikes twelve midnight, indicating the time to start eating the grapes. (Before that you **must** find a place to safely put down your glass of cava — the Spanish version of Prosecco or bubbly wine.)
- The bell starts to ring in the New Year, and you eat one grape each time the bell strikes. (That may seem simple but when you get to the fifth or sixth bell, those grapes get tougher to swallow.)
- You must eat (and swallow) all twelve grapes before the bell has finished its toll. (That's not easy to do with those thick skins and seeds — not like the soft, sweet and seedless variety we get at home.)
- After the twelve bells are finished, everyone goes around to hug and give sticky, juicy grape kisses.

Vispera de Año Nuevo!!

After the grape-eating extravaganza, we walked *en masse* to a nightclub, where the party kept going. However, I just kept walking — back to the apartment I shared with Melissa G. – where I tucked myself into bed after the long transition day. This New Year was going to be a good one!

THE MORNING AFTER

Everyone arrived in various states of recovery at the restaurant, Casa Clemencia, for our New Year's Day brunch of *paella*, the dish made famous by Valencia (another go-to meal of the month.)

With our bellies full, we wandered out onto the streets, fascinated by the oranges growing on the main streets of the city! **Wow!** That's amazing. They **are** Valencia oranges, so surely they would be tasty, right? Wrong. Poor Mark discovered that these oranges are the sourest of citrus.

These are not the sweet, GMOd perfection of the Valencia oranges we were brought up with in North America — those Valencia oranges are a hybrid created in California in the mid-19th century. *These* Valencia oranges are just for show. We should have asked the all-knowing Claire first.

CLAIRE'S STOMPING GROUNDS

Claire's infectious smile, ever-present energy and positive vibes have kept us sane through the first half of our trip. She is our rock, the person we go to when we're lost or confused or need some moral support. She's a perfect balance of masculine and feminine, right and left-brain — the queen of logistics with a heart of gold. So when she offered up this month's Positive Impact project, I was a definite **yes**!

During the many years she was living in Valencia, she walked the dogs at the local shelter, and during our visit we were honored to join her. I wondered if the dogs spoke Spanish. I must admit it wasn't the most glamorous way of giving back, and to be honest I was a little scared of the barking, howling, stressed-out, rambunctious K9s. It was very sad to see those poor pups caged and crazed, but it felt good to support them and Claire's cause as she had supported us in ours.

Social Hack

Do something uncomfortable to give back to someone who has helped you. It doesn't take much to sacrifice a few hours. Who do you know who has supported you along the way? How might you show your appreciation by giving back to something that is important to them?

CHECK THAT BUCKET LIST

There is one city I have wanted to visit since I was a teen, when I heard about it from friends who did that after-high-school-self-discovery-travel-through-Europe. I never had a chance to do that — it just took a little longer for me.

I felt such HAPPINESS visiting my #1 bucket list destination — Barcelona and the Sagrada Familia, Gaudi's architectural dream-come-true. This unique and holy wonder is an elegant tapestry of science and nature. Gaudi looked at nature for inspiration and used sacred geometry to create some of its magnificent detail.

A day spent inside this building brings you awe and a spirited connection to God. It's the most beautiful building I've ever seen. You can imagine the COURAGE it must have taken Gaudi to create such a thing and the commitment he had to realizing his dream.

His sanctuary in the city is still under construction and is slated to be finished in 2026, the centennial of Gaudi's death. I could work with that timing. Barcelona is actually still on my list because I had to work 1½ days of the three days there.

Bucket List Hack

My visit to Barcelona after all these years, and my experience at the Sagrada Familia, reminded me how important it is that we realize our dreams. It may not always be easy, and we may need to fight hard to get what we want, but our dreams are worth it on so many levels. It may take a lot longer than you imagine, but if it's important to you and others, then commit to it.

Remember, COURAGE is not always about taking a great stand; sometimes COURAGE is about sticking to what is right for you, even if you are experiencing obstacles.

Don't be afraid to create your own outrageously exciting bucket list — whether it's going on safari in Africa or walking on the Great Wall of China — you have the FREEDOM to make your own choices.

Maybe it's something a little less grandiose, something a little more local. The simple act of writing it down on your bucket list starts to make it a reality. Committing your intention to paper actually activates a part of your brain that can make it happen. Make regular time to build on that dream, even in your imagination. Use positive reinforcement to build up the energy behind it.

Time spent on pursuing your bucket list is not a pipedream or a lark, no matter what that gremlin voice in your head says. Simply ask yourself, "How might I make this happen?" Then be playful in coming up with ways you might be able to do it. You have a responsibility to yourself to follow your heart, create your own joy. Nobody else can do that for you.

I think this quote, which has been attributed to a number of different people, captures the sentiment perfectly: "The brave may not live forever, but the cautious don't live at all." Finding your COURAGE will help you check those life-changing trips off your bucket list.

BETTER TO BE SAFE THAN SORRY

Barcelona is known as the pickpocket capital of the world, with over 300 incidents reported daily. That might well be because the estimated 32 million people who visit each year are wandering around in awe, and not paying attention to what's going on around them.

Poor Laura became one of those stats while traveling on the Metro with her rolling suitcase and her purse perched on top. A team swarmed her to "help with the luggage" and left with her wallet. Some help they were — not a nice introduction to this beautiful city.

Safety is integral to your dream travel. Whether it's keeping your belongings or your person safe, you can never be too diligent. It seems like common sense but sense is not always that common. Although it seems obvious to me, I feel I have to include some travel safety advice.

Safety Hack

No matter where you go in the world, always wear your bag close to your body. Make sure it's sealed with a zipper or other closure that is difficult to open. Carry your bag, pouch, even your knapsack on the front — it may look goofy but really, who cares?

Get a deep cross-body bag with a strong webbing strap (skinny straps can be cut) that's big enough to hold what you need but hard to reach into. This may be a hassle when trying to reach for your camera, your phone or your wallet, but it's more of a hassle when someone else gets it. Don't leave your bag hanging on the back of a chair in a restaurant or rest it anywhere out of reach or eyesight.

There has been a staggering rise in mobile phone theft since people are using their mobile phones more to take pictures and navigate their way through the streets in new environments — or staggering home drunk from a bar (not naming any names here in Spain!) In fact, thieves are always looking for victims who are visibly distracted and will even create the distraction, as was the case with Laura.

Cell Phone Safety Hack

If you need to use your phone out in public, stop and hold it tightly with two hands, and close to your body if possible. Check your directions or take your pictures, then put it away in a secure place. If you don't create the opportunity, you can prevent the crime. Whenever you hit the streets or go to music festivals or ride public transit, you must keep your wits about you.

There is no room for diversion when it comes to your precious cargo. Keep your eyes moving, be aware of your surroundings and the people. Thieves will be thwarted if you appear to be very attentive. Look at the people, not just the attraction. Don't use your cell phone in transit if you don't have to. Check your belongings to make sure everything is secure, and hold on to your stuff when passing through crowded areas. Attention is your best prevention.

Being safe shouldn't prevent you from doing things. In fact, it actually gives you the COURAGE and FREEDOM to do more things than you could ever imagine.

OLD WORLD WORKING

I was working long hours in Spain. January is one of those

months, like September, when my clients have big plans. So I spent many days inside my apartment or at the WayCo shared working space, about a 20-minute walk through the Old Town.

It's easy to start feeling immobilized when the sedentary work life sets in, making it even more difficult to drum up the energy to add tourism and track events to the schedule. We were fortunate to have the Central Market and the UNESCO World Heritage Old Town right across the street from our apartment.

However, Valencia has so much more to offer, with its *flamenco* shows, walking tours and *tapas* tastings. Their inner city urban park (a dried-up river bed) is the largest in Europe and leads to the spectacular City of Arts and Sciences — the most beautiful modern architectural environment I've ever seen.

And the **beaches**! The coastline offers several to the north and south, as well as the biggest one, Playa de la Malvarrosa, close to the centre of the city. They stretch wide and long, and offer an open, friendly and casual place to hang out — when the weather is good. We were lucky to have some warmer days to enjoy a stroll along the sandy shores.

If you are lucky enough to be in Valencia in mid-March, then you will be consumed by the fiery displays of Les Fallas — one of the biggest festivals in Spain. The tradition started when carpenters celebrated the end of the short, cold winter months by burning the wood that held their candles.

Over time, these pieces of wood were painted as playful satirical effigies of local politicians or celebrities, placed around the city and burned as a statement. It wasn't long before those little pieces of wood turned into massive *ninots* — enormous figures made of wood, cardboard, polyurthane, stryofoam, cork, plaster and *papier-maché*. You can imaging the fire hazards!

When the tradition was getting out of hand, the government made it a celebration of San José, the patron saint of carpenters, so that they could lay down some guidelines and manage the crowds that swarmed in from across Spain and the world.

I loved Valencia for its passion and places. It was a great city to mark the end of our European leg and the halfway point of our year. It was hard to believe that it had already been six months! This raised a sense of urgency and determination to get as much in as humanly possible during this time.

GIVE ME MORE

There was **so** much more of Spain to see, and I was leaving a week early for a gig in Cleveland, before stopping in Toronto during our transition to Mexico City. Did I have the energy to squeeze in even more? I had never been to Spain before, and I didn't know when I'd ever be back again. This FREEDOM mindset helped me drum up the COURAGE to stretch even further.

So during the evenings while binging on the new Netflix series, *The Crown*, I researched a road trip to the south of Spain. Then I managed to convince Shruti to join me.

Hey there, little reptilian brain, prepare yourself for a whirlwind weekend tour of Seville, Granada and Rock of Gibraltar on the southernmost tip of Europe, with enough time to take in the sunset on the sandy beach on the west coast in Tarifa. With a view to Morocco to the south, it felt as if our European adventure had come full circle.

It was a long weekend extravaganza, which checked off a few more bucket list items — some I didn't even know I had — although it would have been so much more enjoyable if it were summer time. I'll never forget that night in Granada when Shruti and I huddled around that stupid little electric heater — too cold to sleep, too cold to go out — laughing at the ridiculousness of our situation. It's funny how you remember little moments like that.

FEEL THE FEAR AND DO IT ANYWAY

It's no surprise that this chapter emerged with COURAGE and safety as common bedfellows. When you strike out to tackle your bucket list, it takes a combination of both. There's no sense in being reckless or irresponsible, but you also need to push the edges of your comfort zone.

Life Hack

COURAGE doesn't always roar like a lion. Sometimes it's a nagging little voice that says "do this thing!" Listen to that tiny little voice. Not the reptilian brain that keeps you on the couch, but that insistent little voice that calls you to do greater things.

Over the past few months I've been taking some random Spanish classes with Laura. In Spain — it was time to get serious — *más lecciones* (more lessons). It takes a lot of COURAGE to practice a new language with minimal vocabulary. It requires letting go of self-judgment and just not caring what other people think. You have to be able to laugh at yourself.

In some cases it's a necessity, because nobody speaks English. I also discovered that there are different types of Spanish. In Spain they speak very fast. So there was no way of knowing what the housekeeping staff was trying to tell me.

Even Google Voice Translate was having a hard time picking it up, so I didn't feel so bad.

Though it was frustrating at times, I kept up my lessons. I thought I would have an easier time with my Spanish in Mexico the next month, as I'm more familiar with Mexican Spanish from my years of traveling there. They speak a lot slower.

But first, a little trip home to see my family and friends.

Adiós España

TORONTO TRANSITION

The last six months seemed a blur.

With a little foresight and advanced planning, I was able to stop over in Toronto for ten days before heading to Mexico at no additional charge. Since the Remote Year fee includes the cost of our travel between cities, a simple rerouting took me home.

But then something interesting happened. I was invited to be a subject matter expert at a brainstorming session for a major automotive manufacturer — ironic, considering that I get so much enjoyment out of road trips.

My reroute to Toronto was rerouting once again so that I could spend a couple of days at the Crawford Auto-Aviation Museum in Cleveland, Ohio. All I had to do was come up with ideas to guide their global brand strategy. It validated my love for travel and allowed me to share the physical, mental, emotional, social and spiritual values of a driver from a very personal perspective. Add to that the opportunity to inspire others to embrace the almighty road trip! What a great gig!

Feeling very self-assured at the end of the sessions, I headed home oozing with creative juices — a welcome exhilaration considering I would have been happy to stay home out of sheer exhaustion.

With my creative juices still flowing, I was enthusiastic to start recording the on-camera shots for our *"Video Wisdom NEED-TO-KNOW Video eLearning Series"* I've been working on with my partner, Diane. We combined my expertise in instructional design and marketing with Diane's video mastery to help our clients develop profitable online courses using professional video production.

We had started this project before I left, and each month we chipped away at it. With the scripts for each video complete, she had everything in her studio ready for my week home. Hair and makeup done, teleprompter at the ready, set prepared, lights, camera — action! It was a very full day, shooting the five intros and closing segments for the series. All went well. You can check it out here: www.videowisdomstudios.com/video-e-learning-studio/ Sign up to see the whole series.

TIME TO REPACK

This halftime stopover also allowed me to reassess what I was dragging around the world. Every time I unpacked and repacked my suitcase, the same things I never used came out and went back in again.

Now was the time to unload that unnecessary burden. Yes, I had needed a bunch of professional clothes for my presentations in South Africa and the odd sessions I led in Europe, but the second half of my trip was to be quite different. It was focused on achievement travel — sharing top spot on my bucket list: hiking the Inca Trail up to Machu Picchu.

The apex of the next six months would lie at the top of Machu Picchu, so a wardrobe reconfiguration was in order. Out with the bulky cosmetics, bottles and bags of silly-sundry-maybe-one-day things. Then out to shop for the perfect hiking boots, backpack and outdoor gear for my five-day Inca Trail hike.

In the midst of all of this I heard from Nathan, who was coordinating a trip for 35 of us to Bolivia in May, that we needed Yellow Fever shots in order to get into the country. **What?!**

In a panic, I booked an appointment at the travel clinic on my last day in Toronto. They recommended not only Yellow Fever, but Malaria, Tetanus, Typhoid, Hep A, Hep B, C, D, E, F ... and who knows what else. It's not as if there was any pressure, but when they waved those maps of the countries I've never been to in front of my face, self-preservation kicked in and I made some irrational decisions.

I'm all too familiar with Mexico, so I agreed to the emergency gastro antibiotics. I'd never been to South America before, and we all know that on the first visit to a region, the fear of the unknown is larger than life. So after reviewing and agreeing to all the shots and medicines, I left the clinic hopped up on meds and down on a mortgage-payment-sized-bill on my VISA card. In hindsight I would not do that again.

Travel Med Hack

I'm no doctor, but those generic country maps that inform the clinicians are far too broad. An entire country cannot be affected by malaria. Every country has cities, and even on the edges of the Amazon where you are most likely going to travel, the malaria mosquito is very rare. Go ahead and buy them if you can afford to, but I threw them out at the end of my trip — a costly lesson.

Altitude sickness pills are another interesting contribution from the medical mafia. The natives have had this figured out for centuries — coca leaves, water and cardio exercise.

Sure there were times up in Cusco when I woke up gasping for air, but it was nothing a cup of coca tea and a few deep belly breaths couldn't resolve. More on that later.

Check your home health insurance in advance of traveling to see what inoculations are free through your doctor. Make sure to get the emergency antibiotic for travelers' diarrhea, especially if your destinations have questionable water supplies — like Mexico City or Morocco.

Month 7: Magical Mexico

Destination: Canada – Toronto; Mexico, Mexico City ~ February

Heading south from Toronto's brisk temperatures to the comfy climate of Mexico. Inspiring and eclectic, busy and bizarre, massive and magical — Mexico City was everything I thought it would be and a whole lot more than I bargained for. Just when you least expect it, something appears out of thin air to restrict your FREEDOM of movement.

After some quality time with my family and a few welcome-home gatherings, I was eager to discover the creative inspiration in Mexico City.

It's been on my bucket list since Leonardo DiCaprio and Claire Danes played in the 1996 alternative warring-mafia-empire version of Romeo and Juliet. I was so fascinated by the modernized adaptation of this film, it struck me that Mexico City was *the* Latin American Mecca of creativity. I was not disappointed.

With my visit home and an early departure for Colombia at the end of the month, I only had 2½ weeks to live in the largest city in the western hemisphere. The Greater Mexico City population is over 21 million people, with close to 9 million in the city proper. That's a lot of people, and a lot of interesting stuff to see.

In the whirling, swirling world of work and Europe and home, I had no time to spend on my travel planning. Remember my theory of traveling three times — the one I shared with you back in Prague? Well the first step totally eluded me this month, so I arrived fully dependent on the Remote Year track events and my fellow travelers to offer up some interesting options.

Our central hub in Mexico City was Publico Trabajo. It was a very funky four-storey building with an awesome rooftop, tucked away in Roma Norte neighbourhood just a few blocks from the apartment I shared with my fave roomie, Lee.

I loved working from Publico. The multi-level rooftop deck was a great place to hang out, and it was wonderful that the weather was hot enough to enjoy it. The only downside was the upstairs climb (no elevator), which really made me feel the lack of oxygen at the altitude of 2,250 metres above sea level. Some days I stayed home to work unless I was meeting one of my Remote clients at the workspace.

A CURATOR AT WORK

A couple of days after I arrived, Lee invited me to join her at the Zona Maco Contemporary Art Fair, the most important art fair in all of Latin America, at the massive Centro Banamex inside the Hipódromo de las Américas. There we had the honor of joining her friends who were literally shopping for art for their 21C or Century21 chain of boutique contemporary art museum hotels.

The fair was full of artists from all over the world, displaying the ultimate FREEDOM of creative expression. It was incredible. We walked around with the hotel owners and their art curator to find potent and potential pieces for their collection. They not only looked, but they bought. I appreciate art but have never approached it from a buyer's perspective, so it was a novel experience.

They had a budget that they *had* to spend every year on art, which is a brilliant way to showcase the pieces in their hotels.

Their tastes were daring and delightful: everything from a two dimensional, detailed painting of a Persian carpet to a 20-minute semi-erotic video for movie nights. Then there was the German artist's concept installation that demonstrated how society is stuck in a never-ending cycle on the road to nowhere — using an actual treadmill with a tumbleweed, nudged along with a fan, rolling endlessly back and forth! I couldn't believe they bought it!

Having the good fortune to buy art is a whole other level of FREEDOM. Can you imagine having the COURAGE to buy art worth tens or hundreds of thousands of dollars? This experience struck just the right note to start my creative tour of this fabulous city.

CREATIVITY STEEPED IN CULTURE

The ancient history of Mexico includes five major civilizations: the Olmec, Maya, Teotihuacan, Toltec and Aztec, and provides lots of inspiration to draw from. One of the unique expressions of Aztec folklore envisioned by Mexican architect Javier Senosiain is the Quetzalcoatl's Nest, tucked away inside the suburban neighbourhood of Naucalpan.

Our intrepid explorer, Mikko, revealed one of Mexico City's best kept secrets. Mikko makes it his purpose to dig up some of the most off-the-beaten-track experiences around the world. He scored big-time with this spot, a massive 150-hectre property with only a small portion landscaped to perfection. The artfully manicured gardens and mosaic tile covered benches, tunnels and caves all created a nature-inspired home for the Aztec serpent God, Quetzalcoatl.

This lush hilly haven is interrupted by occasional appearances of the serpent emerging from under the earth and disappearing behind the next bush or hill. The architect's vision was to integrate the existing terrain to enhance the free flowing energy of the environment. The results were unforgettable.

And you can actually stay here! The most prominent portion of the serpent's body contains ten separate apartments spread over 165,000 square feet, one of which is a four-bedroom apartment that accommodates ten guests. It can be rented for only US$250 a night on Airbnb — definitely worth putting on the bucket list.

Creative Hack

Creativity needs constraints. It is a process of allowing meaningful expression to emerge. Whether you are designing a piece of art, a garden or your life, along the way decisions have to be made. Without some type of constraint or guiding criteria it's impossible to determine if your design is unfolding the way you want.

With no vision or personal perspective, the proverbial blank canvas can be stifling. The artist's ultimate challenge is to balance FREEDOM of creative expression within the limits of the medium. It may seem like an oxymoron, but the tighter the restraints; the more creativity is required to be truly innovative.

Regardless of any skills or artistic talent, it's good to develop the artist's mindset – be curious, be brave, be enterprising, be relentless, embrace failure and learn the lesson, see the big picture and pay attention to the details, have a point of view and take time to ponder.

THE TORTURED AND TALENTED ARTIST

One cannot mention Mexico in the context of art without talking about Frida Kahlo — the timeless, uni-browed darling of Mexico's art community. Her story is one of passion, fortitude and unbreakable commitment to her art, the ultimate therapy to distract her from a lifetime of physical pain from a back injury she sustained in an accident in her teenage years.

Her drive to use art as a way to deal with her pain, and her flamboyant, outspoken style and prolific output of paintings, guaranteed her spirit a place in eternity. The Blue House was Frida's paradise and prison, as her life deteriorated to a painful end at 47 years old. I was lucky to visit her home, now a museum, just before closing after a precarious inner city bike ride to the Coyoacán neighbourhood with my trusty sidekick, Lee.

Mexico City inspired the artist within me. When I was younger I promised myself that some day I would retire and study art somewhere in France or Italy. Mexico City has now become a serious contender. Now I just have to figure out how I'm going to retire. For the time being I'm super inspired for my client's graphic design projects. Lucky clients.

SOMETHING FOR EVERYONE

Mexico City has hundreds of galleries and about 150 museums focused on everything from fine art to vintage toys. The Museum of Anthropology is one of the most impressive.

The building is gorgeous and once you get past the bones of primate evolution, the cultural collections and geographic displays provide incredible insight into Mexico's mystical past. Many of the ancient traditions are still practiced throughout Mexico, and not just for the entertainment of tourists.

MARKET MADNESS

One of our track events took us on the Metro to the massive Sonora Central Mercado — a ten square block extravaganza containing Mexico's largest esoteric market. In a culture that is steeped in religion, there is something for everyone — potent herbal intentional concoctions, magical soaps, even voodoo dolls, along with effigies and saints of all descriptions.

There's even a patron saint of drug dealers — Santa Jesus Malverde, a suave looking gent with slick black hair and prominent brows. This is not surprising for a culture that also celebrates the Day of the Dead — their unique expression of All Saints Day and Halloween.

Their devotion to spirit was intoxicating, and contrary to the way I was brought up with absolutely no religious practice. In fact, my father forbade me to attend church until he found out he could get free childcare at the Sunday school. He made me promise not to listen to a word they said. I was a very obedient child.

Then, in my early 20s, I started seeking a truth that was bigger then me. I looked at many different religions and settled on Buddhism — a practice that made the most sense to me. All that said, it's evident to me from looking at the ancient and modern cultural practices in Mexico that it really doesn't matter what you believe in. What matters is that you believe in something.

Spiritual Hack

Even if you were raised to believe in a certain God or relate to a spirit in a certain way, it's okay to update your practice to align with your transforming values. What worked for you or cultures in the past may no longer be relevant. There is a very close link between spirituality and creativity.

For Frida, painting brought her closer to God. Whatever you call your God — Holy Spirit, Elohim, Allah, Krishna or the Light — you were meant to live fully into your creative expression. Reflect what that means for you. Find the spiritual practice that suits your unique soulful needs and brings you HAPPINESS, and then be religious about your practice.

MONARCH MIGRATION

Being in relationship with nature is also a form of spiritual practice. A pilgrimage in nature can evoke an enlightened moment if you keep your heart and mind open.

Growing up in Ontario, I had heard that our beautiful summer Monarch butterflies migrated south to Mexico in the winter. It was a gift to find out that their seasonal breeding grounds were a short pilgrimage away by bus, taxi and an hour tethered horse ride up a mountain.

It took us a couple of hours to arrive at the top of this dusty mountain path, but it was worth every minute. There are no words to describe what it's like to be swarmed by Monarch butterflies, watch them procreate at your feet or silently observe millions of them weighing down the branches of the same tree they come back to every year.

There is magic in nature and we are part of it. Embrace that beautiful side of yourself. A day with the monarchs was a blessing beyond my wildest imagination.

HANGING WITH MONTEZUMA

Even though I prayed to Saint Christopher, the patron saint of travelers, I still succumbed to *Montezuma's Revenge*! Perhaps it was the *mezcal* tastings and *margarita* madness, the community guac-off and *taco* challenges, food trucks and a wide variety of culinary experiences. Or maybe it was simply soaking our homemade meals in the tap water with not enough iodine.

Whatever the cause, one evening on the way back from dinner with Melissa G., the dreaded revenge struck, and I couldn't get home fast enough. That was the beginning of my two-week futile fight. I was fine if I didn't go far — part of the reason I chose to work from home some days. Sitting still was better, so walking around to check out more of the city was not an option.

Thanks to the city's extensive Hop-On-Hop-Off bus network, I was able to squeeze in more sites without the constant search for a bathroom. Over two days, I clenched my way along all three of their routes — the best money I spent that month.

Unfortunately, when the bus driver took a break I wandered a little too far, and returned to the stop only to see the bus driving away! I refused to be caught in this quaint little square, so I ran with all my might. It was three blocks in full sprint before an oncoming pedestrian flagged down my bus and I returned safely to my seat for the rest of the trip. Thank God I did — that was the last bus of the day!

Travel Hack

Even if you're not squeezing your cheeks, the HOPO is a great way to get oriented in a city. I've bought a ticket in most cities I've visited. I recommend hopping on early in the day for the whole route first, then going around the second time to hop off at the places that pique your interest. If the city is big enough, it's worth the two- or three-day deal so that you can spend more time at your favorite places. It's amazing how quickly a day goes by when there is so much to see.

Ironically, given my condition, this was the month that Samvida and Mike held one of their *Healthy Habits for Travelers* workshops, so I decided to apply some holistic measures. But even straight shots of ginger juice couldn't wrestle this bug to the ground. Remember those antibiotic pills I told you to carry with you? This is the time to take them.

Health Hack

It's a wise move to have a preventative approach to your gut health, Samvita offered up these practices.

- *Hydrate with bottled water – clean water is essential. It's key to helping your body deal with issues like altitude, nausea, diarrhea because it helps the body carry more oxygen to vital bodily functions.*
- *Drink your greens. It's hard to get your daily quota of fresh fruits and vegetables. Invest in a light-weight smoothie maker. Then find the local market and load up. Don't forget*

to check the electrical current and outlet style of your destination country. Anything with a motor needs the right electrical currency converter.
- Use these natural preventative remedies to keep your body in good function.
  - Ginger is an antioxidant and anti-inflammatory that helps with indigestion, nausea, drying out mucus and it has anti-blood clotting properties. It also can help with pain. Chop or grate into water and boil to make a tea — a great remedy for colds or stomach issues. Cook with it often.
  - Lemon is full of Vitamin C and great for immunity building. It alkalizes the body — keep in mind many health issues thrive in an acidic environment. The best way to consume lemon is fresh-squeezed in a glass of warm water first thing in the morning.
  - Turmeric is a natural antibiotic and anti-inflammatory that prevents allergies, cold, throat infections, and it can be applied directly to wounds. It can be used in its powdered form in cooking veggies, or added to hot water to make tea.
  - Probiotics are good gut bacteria that crowd out the bad bacteria in our digestive system. This contributes to overall gut health, digestion and absorption preventing digestive, immune, autoimmune conditions and skin issues. A great natural source of probiotics can be found in kombucha (fermented tea), apple cider vinegar (organic, unfiltered, raw less processed), fresh yogurts/kefirs and supplements.

Staying healthy on your travels makes life so much easier.

I was sad to leave Mexico City. Although I won't miss the water, I loved the inspired creativity and eclectic mix of cultural contrast. Mexico definitely added to my HAPPINESS quotient.

It's time to move on to Colombia. That's Colombia, not Columbia. Where you don't have to worry about the water.

Muchas gracias, Ciudad de Mexico

Month 8: Colombian Coffee is the Cure

Destination: Colombia – Barranquilla, Bogota ~ March

Riding the emotional rollercoaster in the theme park of life — on a HAPPINESS high at carnival, then falling down, down, down like the rain in Bogota. It was a month full of celebrations and challenges but isn't that just life in general? Maybe it's a little harder to handle on the road, but nothing some sweet Colombian chocolate can't fix.

Colombia started out on a high. Laura, our native of Barranquilla, had rallied a number of Remotes back in Croatia to join her for the carnival festivities at the end of February — the second largest carnival in the world, surpassed only by Rio in Brazil. Never having attended a carnival, I was eager to participate.

Carnival Barranquilla was everything Laura described — multiday parades, all night parties and people from all over the world celebrating together! She had participated in carnival since she was four years old and, inspired by her grandma, danced in five parades over the years.

Laura knew the drill, and it was a thrill. We had prime seats on the parade route with a cover to protect us from the sun. We danced in the bleachers like-no-one-was-watching to the traditional *cumbia* band, while we waited for the parades to start. The crowds were overflowing with HAPPINESS as people laughed and sang and danced.

Happiness Hack

Dance has been proven to be an effective intervention to improve your short-term and long-term quality of life. Moving our bodies in a rhythmic motion to music integrates our visual, auditory and kinesthetic systems. Dance brings your body in union with your soul, which helps you to feel more HAPPINESS in your life.

Hey, why not just get up and dance for a bit? Nobody can stop you. It just takes a little bit of COURAGE but once you feel the FREEDOM of movement you might get hooked on the HAPPINESS!

DANCE 'TIL YOUR HEART'S CONTENT

Every year the carnival begins on the Saturday before Ash Wednesday and continues until the last man standing at end of the day on Tuesday. Every day there is a parade, each one focused on a different theme.

Saturday is the Battle of the Flowers, the most important and oldest parade held in Barranquilla. It started in 1903 to honor the end of the 1000-day war and the reactivation of carnival celebrations.

Sunday is the day for the Great Parade, introduced in 1967, filled with folkloric dancers and traditional music.

Monday's main event is the Great Fantasy Parade, which was introduced in 2003. I'll leave it to your imagination what characters showed up in that parade.

You can only imagine the colourful and provocative costumes, dancing to music that only the Colombian fantasy can muster up. The moves, the makeup, the money that goes into these festivities is incredible.

Tuesday is the final day. Folklore tells of a drunk and tired man, fondly named Joselito Carnaval, who went missing at the end of carnival. To this day the end of the celebrations are marked by the announcement of his burial — a sad day for the people of Barranquilla.

I'm pretty sure I took over 1,000 pictures that weekend.

BACK TO WORK — AT THE BEACH!

At the beginning of the year, a small group of Ikigais — Anu, Ben, Brian, Gerry, Karen, Lucy and Marko — started a tongue-in-cheek mockery of remote workers and the ridiculous places they prop up their laptops to work. They called it *Digital Douchebag* or DDB, for short. At first it was just a few folks with a broken laptop setting up insane scenarios to bring humour to digital nomads who took themselves way too seriously. Then it became an Instagram sensation. Now Anu, Dan and Jenna maintain a growing collection for over 2,000 followers and contributors — which leads me to our next stop.

Exhausted from all the carnival activities, it was time to head to the beach and get some work done! A bunch of us carnival folks went off to Cartagena to recover and to wait it out for the rest of the Ikigais to join us from Mexico City for our start date in Bogota at the beginning of March. Melissa G. and I relaxed into a gorgeous apartment overlooking the ocean and got back to work — DDB style. There is nothing like that feeling of FREEDOM you get when working from a hammock overlooking the ocean with the breeze gently rocking you back and forth.

CARTAGENA'S CALLING

Although work we must, we made time to discover the beautiful old colonial town of Cartagena with its gorgeous stone buildings and incredible inner courtyards. For a country that has an unsafe reputation, which it's desperately trying to repair, Cartagena has long been a haven for American tourism. There are far too many overpriced shops and restaurants for my liking, but the Free Walking Tour guide revealed some of her best-kept secrets for living like a local.

Travel Hack

The first thing to do when you arrive in any city (after your Hop-On-Hop-Off bus tour) is to attend a Free Walking Tour, if one is available. It's good to research this in advance. These tours are organized daily and are really free, although you are encouraged to tip, as you see fit.

The people who lead the tours are often students who do this to make some money on the side. Their enthusiasm in sharing their knowledge of the city is infectious. They most often have grown up there and are studying history or some related socio-economic topic.

It's a great opportunity to get the lay of the land in a more concentrated area and ask specific questions to plan your meals or other adventures. Check with individual organizations. Some require a pre-booking. You could even ask if there is an opportunity to visit or dine with a local to see what life is really like.

DIETING ON THE ROAD

March 1st arrived and marked my commitment to start the "Whole 30" diet. Let's face it, there's nothing like a good bout of digestive issues to start you off on a new dietary regime. Really I was hoping to just shed a few more pounds.

This food regime eliminates all sugar, alcohol, grains, legumes and dairy. Basically you are limited to vegetables and protein – eggs, chicken, fish and beef. Hopefully it's all organically fed with no antibiotics or growth hormones. It's similar to a lot of other diets that promote healthy, clean eating with no processed foods.

It was a great way to optimize my digestive system and build up those much needed immunities for my upcoming trek to Machu Picchu. A little group of Ikigais had formed as a support system, so I was committed and accountable. Colombia was certainly the perfect place to do this, with its lush, fertile agriculture.

You would think that going on a diet would be difficult while travelling. It is if you think it is. But once you engage in the process, things start to get easier. Certainly once you get over the three-day hump of giving up sugar and wheat, you are more repulsed by it than crave it. Starting in Cartagena and continuing into Bogota, I was adamant I would stick with the plan.

ACHIEVEMENT TRAVEL

For some folks, traveling is a huge achievement. Some travel to visit family or friends. Some travel as an escape from their dreary lives, while others travel for bragging rights to say they've been there, done that. For me, travel is intrinsically linked to achieving a specific goal. That's my "Why" and in this case it was to reach Machu Picchu on the Inca Trail.

Achieving that goal was the motivation that kept me on track with the diet. It took a lot of COURAGE to stick with the program but *I did it!* By the end of March, I had lost over 10 lbs, feeling great and energized.

Physical Hack

Like anything in life, you only achieve results if you commit to a goal. The motivation you need to sustain your behaviour over a long period of time lies in your desire to reach that goal. That goal needs to be "non-optional" — something you can't live without or to which you have committed wholeheartedly. What is it that you really, really, really want to do — and why?

If your "Why" is not strong enough, it's easy to let go of the goal and the behaviour required to achieve it. So when you set a physical goal (or any other goal for that matter) ask yourself "Why, do I want this?" Ask "Why?" until you cry to get to the deepest source of motivation within you. Then start making the plan to get there. When you hit the hard parts, revisit your "Why?" And make sure you have a support system in place to help you along the way.

COFFEE TALK

Thank goodness the diet didn't restrict my coffee. We had the most delightful experience attending a coffee tasting with one of Bogota's premier coffee sommeliers, Lucia Londoño. She is of German descent and comes from generations of coffee growers in Colombia. She supplies coffee to restaurants, hotels and businesses. We were honored to taste and select a blend for her new product offering.

We identified the four key coffee characteristics: acidity, aroma, body and aftertaste. Then we did a taste test using that same coffee blend with six different types of coffee makers: Bodum French press, Melita drip filter, airpress,

Chemex pour-over and a syphon method. It was shocking to taste the difference among all these coffee making methods. I was pleased to discover the best tasting one and the one she recommends is the method I've been using for years — the Melita drip. Hmmm — I think I'll go make one right now. Mmmmm — HAPPINESS!

SHOCKING NEWS FROM HOME

I was just getting into the rhythm of Bogota after our first week when I got a call from my sister on a Saturday evening. It wasn't good. My Dad had been admitted to hospital with a heart rate less then 20 beats per minute. We were lucky he was still alive. He had been sluggish for a while and had been falling quite a bit, but he just figured it was old age.

Dad's pulmonary system has had its challenges over the years. First his heart palpitations were rectified with day surgery. Years later my osteopath found an aneurism in his main aorta just in time. Thank God! (His medical doctor would never have found it and refused to recognize osteopathy as a viable alternative, charting that the discovery was made by accident.)

This time the resident doctor at the seniors' complex detected the heart rate issue when my Dad complained about not being able to clear his lungs. Thankfully this diagnosis was easy enough to find and they arranged for an emergency pacemaker surgery. The surgery was scheduled for Monday.

I had to book an emergency flight home the next day to be there in time and take care of my Mom, who has Alzheimers, while he recovered. A last-minute flight was super-expensive, especially flying from South America, and the cheaper options had numerous stopovers, which wouldn't get me there fast enough.

I had just committed a ridiculous amount of money to a month of extreme travel adventures in May. But at the end of the day, it's only money and there's always more where that came from. So I booked it and was off to the airport at 5 am the next day. There is no question when you know what's really important in life.

When I arrived to see my father weak, white as a ghost and fearful for his life, there was no doubt I had made the right decision. The surgery was a success, and the pacemaker would keep my bionic father going! He was given another chance to stick around to care for my Mom, and we were happy to have our Dad around for a while longer.

He sprang back to action with much more energy than before. We got him settled back home and I arranged for my flight back to Bogota ten days later.

The desire to give up on my yearlong folly started to grow with fervor from that moment on. This was the first time since Morocco that I really wanted to quit. It's times like this when COURAGE plays with your emotions, taunting you with yearnings to have or do something other than what you are currently experiencing. I tried to release the feelings; as they rose up, I'd let them go.

Soon after when I heard my Dad's arm was swelling as a result of a blood clot after the surgery, I was having a harder time letting go of the longing for home. To top it off, my son was also going through a tough time and I wasn't there to support him. I was agonizing with guilt, worry and shame — alone, vulnerable and frightened.

What was I doing on the other side of the world? How selfish! How thoughtless! I should be home. These thoughts whipped me. Thankfully, my Dad was prescribed the latest technology in blood thinners, which took care of the blood clot in short order. But unfortunately there was no quick fix for my feelings.

IT CUT THROUGH ME LIKE A KNIFE

Two weeks after my father's surgery and only a few day after my return to Bogota, my sister's husband collapsed from a perforated bowel. The admitting doctor made a bad call that Friday afternoon at 4 pm (she probably had plans for the weekend), which sent him into five days of toxic shock — something no one has ever survived.

If not for his relentless desire to live and his loving family surrounding him every minute of those five days, we would have lost him. Those who are closest to me were all suffering, and I didn't even know what was going on until the dust settled over a week later. I felt helpless. Devastated.

Should I fly back again? My gut was telling me to go, but my sister insisted it wasn't necessary and that he was in no shape for visiting. It would be three months before he would be released from the hospital, then another three months to recover completely.

By that time I would be back from the year. It was the hardest thing I had to do this entire year — to just carry on with my plans, live my life and pray for my family every day from a distance.

I'm sure anyone who lives far away from loved ones can relate to this. As I write this part of the story, Anton, my cousin in The Netherlands, is preparing himself for an early departure. By the time you read this, he will have passed from fibrosis of the lungs at the much too early age of 65. It was a bizarre coincidence that I found out about it at exactly the same time as I'm writing this. (Just had to include that, as I think there are higher energies at work here. Write on.)

Emotional Hack

Whenever you find yourself in times of crisis, remember the Serenity Prayer. "God grant me the serenity to accept the things I cannot change; COURAGE to change the things I can; and wisdom to know the difference."

These words brought me much comfort over the days and weeks that followed. While my family struggled at home, the guilt was overwhelming. My poor sister was left alone to deal with her husband's recovery **and** my parents.

There were many days during the rest of the year when all I really wanted to do was just go home. When I was having a hard time with this, I would say the prayer and go on my way.

GET BACK TO WORK!

In Bogota we worked from two Work&Go offices — one across from the big mall above the Starbucks in ZonaT and other on Calle 95 in Chico Norte. Where we worked depended a lot on where our apartments were relative to these two places.

Although some folks were café workers, whose goals were to find the perfect place to set up, connect and get down to it, I still preferred the dining room table at home. At times like this, though, the home office was far too isolating, so I headed to either coworking space to get a little social time in. But then I'd be too distracted and my productivity suffered, so off I went back home again.

I work from home when I'm in Toronto, so I guess you can take the girl out of the home office but your can't take the home office out of the girl!

Work Hack

It's important to pay attention to your preferred working style before you become a digital nomad. If you are used to working in an office environment and enjoy the social aspects, check out the co-working locations. This is a great way to meet new people and get to know the locals.

Some remote workers find FREEDOM in working at a café. If that's you then chances are that you will continue to seek out café workplaces — of which there is a growing number in digital nomad friendly cities.

Of course, the café is only as good as its internet connection. So be sure to check the connection speeds before ordering your coffee, bubble tea or matcha drink and settling in. Download one of the many Speedtest apps or check out Speedof.me, before heading out. Determine your ideal upload and download speeds based on what you need the internet for.

Test your wifi at home and see what you are used to, as a gauge to seek and sip at the perfect café.

A COUNTRY IN CONFLICT

This month's track events were excellent. I chose the History of Conflict in Colombia. It focused on a country and a people that have been torn apart by drug cartels, guerilla wars and corrupt politicians for decades.

It was fascinating to get the insider view from many perspectives. We watched movies and listened to speakers, talked with locals, historians and advocates for social change. It was an incredibly eye-opening experience to see the various truths behind the propaganda that made its way to our televisions back in the 80s — the news that kept people away from Colombia for so many years.

Our guide from the Free Walking Tour in Bogota begged us to tell our friends that Colombia is not what it used to be. It is a better place, a safer place and a beautiful place, with a proud and passionate people, just waiting to be discovered.

Indeed that is exactly what I experienced. Although I was only in Bogota for a few short weeks, it was just the beginning of my education about Colombia.

Travel Hack

Take the time to learn about the history and not-so-distant past of the places you visit. Listen to the experience of the local people, not just what the tourist agencies or politicians want you to hear.

A BLOOMING INDUSTRY

Colombians take care of each other, especially when others have let them down. It was reassuring to find out that the Colombian floral industry — the second largest flower exporter in the world, next to The Netherlands — has socially conscious hiring practices.

Because of the country's *machismo* culture, many women are left as single moms when their men wander off to sow their wild oats. At least 25% of the staff in the floral industry are single mothers, which ensures that the children of their nation are supported and fed, even when their own fathers are not willing or able to do so.

We spent a day in the Sabana, outside of Bogota, at a flower "factory" learning how millions of chrysanthemums per day make it to homes around the world. It's a fascinating process from small cuttings from the mother plant to planting in tight little rows in a massive building large enough to hold 500,000 seedlings.

Once the roots are established, they are hand placed in soil flats and moved to the next building using tray holders that hang on cable tracks. As the plant grows, it is moved again and again to be pruned, then receive slightly different fertilizers and growing conditions to make it the best bloom it can be — until finally, the flower is ready for market.

It is processed, packed and shipped to its final world market destination within 24-48 hours, kept at exactly 2°C to ensure its freshness – a miracle of nature, orchestrated by humans.

DIVERSITY IN NATURE

Colombia is the most biodiverse country in the world, including a unique biosphere that produces some of the country's freshest water supply. Colombians have a deep connection with nature rooted in their ancestral past.

They also have a natural affinity to gold through the legend of El Dorado (the golden man.) The gold museum in downtown Bogota has a thorough account of this history.

A visit to the volcanic Lake Guatavita, a couple of hours outside the city, holds the mysterious story of the ancient Muisca people, a legend that also revolves around gold.

It is said that during their coronation, each new tribal leader or "zipa" was completely covered in gold and floated to the middle of that lake on a raft. He then plunged in to rinse off the gold as more gold pots, jewels and other gold items were thrown in as an offering to ensure nature would continue to provide the great bounty it had in the past.

It appears to be working, as the Colombian landscapes are breathtaking and well worth more time to explore. We were treated to its splendor during our bus ride transition through the mountains between Bogota and Medellin. Colombia would continue to provide mind-blowing natural beauty from our new location in Medellin.

The ten-hour bus ride gave me plenty of time to reflect on the month. I learned many years ago that when life gets crazy, it's important to keep your sense of humor. This reminds me of the closing ditty from the Monty Python movie, "Life of Brian" — *Always look on the Bright Side of Life* — and the value of the British stiff-upper-lip stoicism when life gets you down. It really does help the HAPPINESS factor.

Month 9: City of Eternal Spring

Destination: Colombia – Medellin ~ April

Just as the title suggests – but with very little rain. Is it possible that one place could be so perfect, or is that just the coffee talking? Hey tall, dark and handsome. There ain't no mountain high enough to keep me from you, Juan Valdez. There's another intoxicating blend of liquid gold just up the next mountain.

I was happy to leave Bogota and some of those challenging moments behind. I was ready for a refreshing change.

I instantly fell in love with Medellin! Along with Lisbon, it was one of my fave cities of the entire year. We lived in a big five-bedroom apartment with an amazing sunset view in El Poblado, an upper class neighbourhood originally built with drug money, which continues to cater to the city's elite as well as increasing tourism.

Many of the apartments in Medellin overlook spectacular vistas. The city runs through a valley, while urban growth creeps up the sides of the mountains on either side. Tall apartment buildings rise high above the city, accessed only by a complicated weave of *calles* and *carreras* (roads and avenues), which neither Uber nor Google maps could ever get right.

Distances were deceiving, especially when walking or cycling to a destination. The valley in the middle has a river running beside the very efficient and spotless transit system. It's illegal to eat food, leave garbage or otherwise disturb the system, and the rules are strict — zero tolerance. This provides a measure of assurance when traveling on public transit in a city that was once known for its extreme violence.

In fact many parts of the city are safe, but as the locals say, *papaya dada, papaya partida*. When papaya is given, papaya is taken.

Safety Hack

"No da Papaya" (Don't give Papaya) is a Colombian expression meaning, don't put yourself in a situation where you might be taken advantage of. Be smart, be aware of what's going on around you and don't mindlessly invite crimes of opportunity.

Travel in a group if you can, know where you are going so that you don't look lost, be discreet — loud or rambunctious behaviour is not only disrespectful, but it draws unnecessary attention. Hold your bags close and your mobile phone even closer. If you're going to take pictures, put the camera strap around your wrist so that it's clear you are being conscious of your safety.

Don't wear your floral Margueritaville shirt and your giant, multi-lens camera around your neck in the city centre near Parque Berrio or any secluded barrio that is off the beaten track. It's not only bad judgment; it really is a bad look!

RECOVERING FROM CRISIS

Tourism took a hit during the Narcos wars in the 80s, and while the government has successfully resurrected the industry, in Medellin there are still some scars that have not healed. Some folks are quite baffled by the presence of foreigners parading around the inner city in large walking tours. Others are tremendously proud of their revival stories.

One such story is the Moravia Walk of Hope. What was once the city's garbage dump became the home of victims who fled the atrocities of guerrilla invasions in the countryside. These people arrived at the north bus terminal and found gold in other people's garbage. With nothing but the clothes on their backs, they scavenged for food and anything they could sell to make a living. And live they did, right there on top of the garbage dump from 1977 to 1984. With the materials that were dumped there each day, shelters were built.

More people came. More homes were built. With the increase in guerilla and paramilitary activities in the rural areas, more people escaped and found their way to Medellin. The dump community grew — at its peak over 17,000 people lived on top of the garbage in fewer than 2000 "homes".

In 2004, government programs started reallocating most of the families into no-cost or low-cost alternative housing, but some still remain. As the government moved people out, they didn't destroy the properties quickly enough, and other folks moved right in and waited for their free homes to come up. The women I met on my visit were proud to be fighting for free homes for themselves and their children. Basically anyone who lived on the dump would get a free home. Crazy!

In 2014, a census revealed there were still 120 families living on the dump. An educated guess would say there are closer to 250 families squatting in the area — and that number is still growing.

Today the old El Morro dump has been transformed. With the collaboration of university research teams, gardens are being planted over the dump to test which plants can not only survive, but are most effective at bioremediation.

At the top of the mound is the peak of social impact, the CoJardinCom gardens, where the women of El Morro dump community grow plants to sell at local markets and government landscaping projects. They are living proof that hard work and collaboration can really mean one man's garbage is another man's gold — or in this case, perhaps another woman's gold.

This was just one of the inspiring stories that endeared me to Medellin — voted the Most Innovative City in the World in 2013.

Their unprecedented Narcos recovery projects extended the transit system into isolated mountainside neighbourhoods, like Commune 13, which can now be reached by cable car and escalator. There, the youth are trained in the arts, allowing them to display their skills instead of getting tangled up in the wicked web of the drug world.

So many lives can change when a mayor, his government and the community have the COURAGE to take on the drug cartels. What an inspiration!

THE POWER OF COMMUNITY

The Ikigai tribe was now a tight community, with some of us floating in and out on the periphery. We created traditions, like Brunch or Die, Game Night and Wisdom Wednesdays, where each person shared his or her experience, expertise or a teachable moment.

Now there was *Tejo* or *turmeque*, Colombia's national sport, which is believed to have origins in the pre-Colombian Muisca tribes. Every week the team got together to toss rocks at a target loaded with gunpowder. Keen shots were rewarded with a blast. What's not to like about that? Our crew took to this explosive sport with a vengeance, and these weekly tournaments pit teams against each other for the ultimate prize: bragging rights.

As we moved from country to country, more rituals were added, like BenEats (eating contest), Magic Dining (high end supper club) and Bebiernes (a linguistic twist for Friday drinks) which started in a sassy, sexy bar in Medellin called La Chiquita. I'm happy to say some of these community events still live on to this day through the beauty of the interweb. Slack and WhatsApp and Zoom room chats keep the community spirit alive.

But it wasn't all fun and games. Tough times hit everyone at some point along the way. Friendships flared and fizzled, romance ignited and withered, but in the end connections made on this journey will last a lifetime.

They say you come for the travel, but stay for the community, and that's true. I found my best travel companion in Lee, the New York City wound-tight, party-all-night super-sales-executive-*cum*-laid-back, simple-life, intrepid travel-blogger. Her reinvention emerged gracefully over the year and I was blessed to share in her adventures.

We lived in our Medellin apartment with Becca and Jacob, and the many visitors who came and went throughout the month. Back in Prague, Lee and I had discovered our common love of home cooking and movies, with a good bar of chocolate to finish off the night. The Colombian chocolate made it even better! We rested up in the evening so that we could rev up the exploration in the daytime.

It was April already and there was less then four months left of this radical year. My attention had shifted from running my business to racing through South America in a desperate attempt to inhale it all. With that shift came a slowdown in my client projects — and the gift of time. I had the sense that if I didn't embrace the FREEDOM of experiencing these countries, I wouldn't have the chance to do it again. So I summoned the COURAGE to enjoy every minute.

There was a lot to see and do in any given day — from exotic fruit tastings, to artisan markets, *guarapo* (sugar cane drink), food festivals and the search for the finest *arepa* — that mouthwatering corn flour cake which *must* be fried, not baked. Oh, and did I mention the coffee?

COFFEE TALK

One of the best things about Colombia is its coffee, which is even better straight from the source. As part of our *From the Earth* track this month, a group of us experienced an authentic Colombian coffee plantation at D'Arrieros Coffee in the Vereda La Aldea, San Sebastián de Palmitas, where we were dressed us up as actual farmers — with white hats, ponchos and red bandanas. Armed with baskets, we ventured up the slopes to pick, peel and process the beans.

While we watched them dry on the rooftop, sipping the fruits of the coffee growers' labor, our charming host pointed off into the distance — up, up, up into the mountains. ***That*** is where we will go this afternoon. I was breathless already and I hadn't even started hiking yet. When I remembered my experience back in Bulgaria, my heart beat faster with the fear that I woudn't be able to make it to the top. We were given the choice of hiking or riding a horse. After weighing the alternatives, I decided the horse was the lesser of two evils.

I confessed to not having ridden a horse in over 30 years (and then only once), so they gave me a mule instead. Even that proved too much to handle.

As the hikers hiked and the riders rode, we started up the steep, twisting and narrow path carved into the side of the mountain. My mule stayed put, pressing me against the grassy bank to the right as the other riders squeezed by on the left — sure-footed on the edge of that precipitous slope.

Panic set in. In an attempt to avoid an unexpected lane change while others moved forward, I pulled back on the reins, not realizing this signaled not only to stop, but to keep moving back. As the mule obediently backed up, I heard our tour guide screaming, "Stop!"

Beep. Beep. Beep. Like a truck with no rearview mirror, I was reversing out of control. We crashed into the hairpin turn behind us, and the sudden stop jolted me off the back end. **Booph!** In a dusty, disheveled mix of embarrassing denial, I pleaded my case. There was no time for that, "Get back on!" retorted the guide.

My eyes darted around for an escape. Perhaps there was still time to ditch the donkey and join the hikers, but he and his huge horse blocked the path below. There was only one way to go: up! And he was not letting me off the hook.

Scared and shaking, I got the COURAGE to lift myself back up. With a little tugging and shifting I slouched into the saddle and surrendered to the situation. As they say, if you fall off the horse (or is that a bicycle?) you have to get back on it. I'm glad I did.

As we clomped up the climb, I sorted out my messy emotions, choosing HAPPINESS over suffering. It wasn't long before we met up with the hikers, standing like cheerleaders around the next corner. The news had already reached them. They were caught somewhere between laughter and concern, wondering how on earth this old gal was going to react. Bless their hearts.

The only thing hurting was my pride — a humbling and humiliating moment. I continued on stoically. Riding up to the top of that mountain was well worth the effort, as the view from the top was awesome — pure FREEDOM.

The torrential rain that hit us on the way back down into the valley — not so much. Soaked to the bone by the end of our ride, we lunched on our traditional homemade tamales while the rain fell sideways on the roadside shelter. We were none the worse for wear, but we sure were glad when the van came to bring us home.

Emotional Hack

You can choose to suffer or your can choose to live and laugh at yourself. In the end, it's all a choice.

HAPPINESS is available to you any time you choose it. It all starts with a smile. As I mentioned back in Bulgaria after my night at the Comedy Club, science confirms that the brain responds to a smile — whether genuine or manufactured — with happiness-inducing chemicals. The more you smile, the more chemicals are released, giving you the feeling associated with that smile. HAPPINESS!

The more you practice the easier it becomes.

Try it now. Start smiling. Now pay attention to what is happening inside your head. Let go of those negative-judgemental-cynical-and-defiant-self-righteous-self-

defeating thoughts. Focus on the smile and let your body relax into it. Let it seep into your consciousness. If your thoughts drift away, bring them back to your smile. Allow the smile to open your heart.

Give yourself permission to live into it, accept it and be happy. Take baby steps every day and before you know it you'll be smiling away.

ANOTHER MOUNTAIN HIGH

The mountain adventures continued. Ana, our local experience lead, put together another insightful day for those of us fortunate enough to get on the coveted *From the Earth* track. Together we ventured up another mountain just outside Medellin to visit Cannaturalia, an authentic artisanal lab that extracts THC and CBD for the medical marijuana market.

Like obedient students in a science class, we listened to Juan, a university marine biology professor, tell us about his dream to support humans and animals with his extracted oils. We watched his scientific slides about different extraction methods used around the world, followed by a demonstration of one of his favorites right there. It was indeed an eye-opening and mind-numbing experience.

PATRON SAINTS AND ACCIDENTS

Mountain highs seemed to be a theme through our adventures around Medellin. Lee arranged another mountain coffee trek for her friend Garvin, who was visiting this month. We were off for a two-day trip to Jardin, a beautiful colonial town south of Medellin.

Those wild, winding country roads require a second driver to navigate around the corners while the bus passes slower cars, trucks and the odd mule pulling a cart.

One abrupt turn jettisoned a glass soda bottle from the overhead compartment — and gravity pulled it with much force directly down onto my head. The pain was excruciating. The owner of the bottle was beside herself with apologies, none of which I was ready to hear or accept. As the egg grew larger on the crown of my head, giant tears streamed down my face. (Funny, I just felt a little tinge of pain as I write this.)

The throbbing continued for the next two hours, as that annoyingly violent ride thrashed our bodies to and fro. I was pissed, and I owned that feeling the whole way. I was not ready to let it go. Laughter — smaughter. I wanted to roll around in my own suffering and self-pity, especially as the physical pain was just too much to ignore. I suppose I could have practiced laughter yoga (which I told you about back in Bulgaria), but it wasn't really appropriate on a bus full of people.

The pain finally subsided when we passed through the little town of Andes. The bus circled back to the highway after collecting more passengers at the bus station, where traditional chiva buses were loading up people and things to take to far-off parts of the surrounding mountains.

I had to crack a smile when I saw this — a statue of the Patron Saint of Accident Victims! Seriously, this is really a thing! It had an angel looking over people caught in a fiery crash at the base. Some were in terror and pain, others already ascending into peaceful bliss — a harsh reminder that things could always be worse.

I'll take a bottle on the head any day.

I did finally forgive the girl when we got off the bus at the main square of Jardin on that beautiful sunny Tuesday afternoon in April. Life goes on, the pain soon forgotten. I was ready for my first stay at a hostel — really! It's just not something I ever did in my travels. A good night's rest prepared us for our trek up to another coffee farm the next morning.

CAN TOO MUCH COFFEE BE DANGEROUS?

The adventure started with an incredible ride in a wooden box cable car at La Garrucha. With only four passengers, it transversed the valley to the place where we continued our trek. Cable boxes like these can be found all over the countryside in Colombia's coffee growing regions. They transport workers and residents across the deep valleys.

One of the gals on our trek was petrified of heights, so it took a lot of COURAGE for her to climb inside one of those buckets. I was so busy consoling her, and holding her hand tightly until the blood drained from mine, that I missed the whole ride!

Once we landed, a lovely walk through the country ended in a serious trek up the mountain that burned my lungs like the roasted coffee beans that awaited us at the top.

Our host, like many local farmers, grows coffee for giant conglomerates like Nespresso. To taste this elixir so fresh from the farm was a euphoric experience. It was well worth the sweat, and even the muddy streaks that were evidence of my fall down the slippery, rain-drenched slope of the near-vertical coffee plantation that afternoon. Exhiler-austed again! We returned to Jardin just in time to catch the bus back to Medellin — past the statue of the Patron Saint of Accident Victims. Thank goodness we didn't have to call on him (or her) on this trip.

NOT *THAT* MOUNTAIN!

There does come a time when you have to say, "No", and that's precisely what I did when the next mountain adventure was looming. I had crashed a track event that included rappelling off a cliff inside a waterfall. (I had intended to let my son take my place, but as it turned out, he wasn't able to visit.)

As the day drew closer, the reality set in. We would be hiking through a mosquito-infested forest to climb up a cliff and dangle from a rope while crashing into a slimy, hard rock face and being bombarded by freezing cold rushing water — only to finish, hopefully unscathed, sopping wet and cold, and hike back on another even more difficult trail.

Maybe I'm just getting way too soft in my old age, but nothing about that seemed appealing. Many of these details I did not know ahead of time. Ignorance is bliss, but sometimes bailing is even more beautiful. If you're going to do something extreme, make sure it's something you enjoy.

MY HARDEST MOUNTAIN TO CLIMB

Back home there were ongoing struggles with my brother-in-law, and the ordeal my sister and family were dealing with was tearing me apart inside. I was feeling very vulnerable, and the desire to abandon the year was welling up like a tsunami. I felt guilty for having a good time while my family was suffering so much. I felt useless.

I was already obsessing about returning home, spending countless hours playing out real estate scenarios in my head. Where would I live? Would I sell or rent out my house? Could I even afford to move back in? My indulgence was racking up a bit of debt, and my clients' projects were drying up like one of those arid Colombian biospheres.

I was in heavy internal debate about whether to finish this folly. In my quiet time, I hit the bottom in an ineffective funk.

Then my phone pinged with a message from Taylor: "Are you still interested in paragliding? It's happening today." The irony was not lost on me. Here was another chance to feel my FREEDOM when the tether of emotion was so firmly attached to home. In the lowest of lows, I knew I had to go. It was the only way out of my funk, so off I went to join the others and fly.

We waited an hour for the van — but it was full. My pity party and I were ready to walk away, but the rest of the group would not hear of it. An extra seat was found for me and we were off into the Medellin mountainside once again. There were a hundred steep stairs to climb to get to the launch pad of Paragliding Medellin.

With every step, my COURAGE was challenged. Higher and higher, the tension grew in the pit of my stomach. Was I really going to hurl myself off a cliff over the city of Medellin? "How reckless! How selfish! How ridiculous!" The voice in my head had a lot to say about this foolishness, but I persevered. I stood in the face of that fear and did it anyway. This time I was committed and content.

I always wanted to fly like a bird. Even in my falling dreams, I would stretch out my wings and be lifted by the draft. This mountain adventure did not include hard rocks and cold water, just warm spring air and someone to strap onto who knew what the hell he was doing. Well let's hope so.

That was Wil, my guy. My young hero for the day was the same age as my son, and there was something beautiful about that. After the short briefing and safety checks, I was saddled up and carried down the gentle grassy slope. Without any effort on my part, the wind picked up the sail and lifted us off the ground.

There are no words to describe my feelings at that moment. I found these in the dictionary: exilient or exultant, jubilant, thrilled, delighted, joyous. Whatever you want to call it, it all came out in squeals of laughter.

OMG! OMG! OMG! I was more elated than I had ever been in my life. Going from depression to elevation injected the experience with even more power. I had found the remedy for when I'm feeling low: get high. Medellin brought me back to life — refreshed and ready to take on the next month of madness.

Life Hack

Sometimes we lack the COURAGE to try new things even though we really want to. Consciously or unconsciously, we put excuses in the way of this FREEDOM. Give yourself permission to do the things you want to do — live the life you want to live. Like everything, it takes practice. Start small and build up to the bigger things.

Month 10: The Full Monthy

Destination: Ecuador, Peru, Bolivia ~ May,

I still find it hard to believe that all of this happened in one month. Back-to-back adventures filled with awe and wonder. Every day took us to a new place with different weather, different people. We were spinning and spiraling through the vortex of time. Planes, trains, buses, vans, cars and carts all carried us to the next destination. Strap yourself in!

I decided to opt out of the Remote Year program for the month of May while the rest of the group was in Lima, Peru. That just meant I would not travel with them, stay in their apartment or participate in the programming for one month. I'd be back together with them in June.

I had to check a few more things off of my bucket list.

Vying for top ranking right up there with Barcelona was Machu Picchu. I was excited that my dear friend from high school, Rada, and her pals Pauline, Michael and Brian, were going with me — my first and only visitors from home all year. It took a bit of coordination, as the Inca Trail needed to be booked back in December. But the time had come and I was psyched to go.

How much could one possibly fit into a month? Well, you're about to find out.

I mentioned that back in January Nathan, our levelheaded, cool-calm-and-collected digital business guru and Bolivian native, had offered up a Bolivian tour. (Remember the yellow fever shots that turned into a mortgage payment's worth of other medications and immunizations?)

The Bolivian adventure was happening at the end of May, which would allow me to rejoin my group in time to head for Argentina in June. The price was right, the itinerary was awesome! Thirty-five Ikigais were committed to this five-day journey to La Paz, Lake Titicaca and the Bolivian Salt Flats — I'm *in*!

It wasn't until I arrived in South America and started to look closely at the map that I noticed how close I was to the Galapagos Islands. It's definitely bucket list worthy but was far-fetched from my home vantage point up in Toronto. It seemed like one of those places you only see on TV.

So I started my Step #1 travel planning. I spent hours researching the options, juggling dates with my Bolivian and Peruvian plans, and figuring out my finances. Then came an invitation to join a few other Remotes on a five-day western island catamaran cruise on the Nemo I.

For a scuba diver and marine wildlife lover like me, it was a no-brainer; for a financially responsible solopreneur in a soft period of business, the cost was a little daunting. I had already struggled with the decision to take the entire month off, but that was back when I was busy with loads of projects. As this month grew closer, the projects and retainer clients grew further away. It's almost as if I was being given the gift of time to make this dream come true.

I then rationalized my decision to go by justifying the thousands of dollars I would save by taking advantage of where I was — a hop-skip-and-a-jump to the Galapagos

Islands, a short plane ride away from Bolivia and a road trip from Cusco into the Amazon Jungle. That's right — an Amazon adventure rounded out the month.

It took a lot of COURAGE to keep putting out cash when there wasn't that much coming in. This is when faith must be strong. I truly believed the money would come — and it did. I'm going for The Full Monthy.

Life Hack

These are not words your financial advisor will ever share, but I think it's important to invest in yourself and your life experience. Playing small gets you nowhere. It only attracts more of the same small energy, people and experiences. Expanding your vision to include a bigger, better reality for yourself enables you to live into that vision.

Is there a nervous Nelly inside of you telling you to stay put and stay safe? That is your amphibian brain doing its job to protect you. It only knows three reactions: freeze, fight or flight. It's the freezing part that will keep you from following your dreams and checking those items off your bucket list. The best way to deal with that little reptile is to say, "Thanks for your concern and support, but I'm going ahead anyway. I'll do my due diligence to make sure we're safe, but you can't stop me from living the life I want to live. So relax and come along for the ride."

The right time will never come, so take the time while you have it. Invest in your dream, whatever it is. Set your intention and ask for the universe to support you in making it a reality. Having the right intention is a powerful thing. Be clear and focused, then commit. Be all in!

LET THE MAY MADNESS BEGIN!

Most of the month was spent in out-of-the-way locations. Traveling in three different countries and far off places, I chose not to get a SIM card, so I was completely dependent on any wifi connection I could find to communicate.

Thankfully my brother-in-law was out of the hospital and on the road to recovery. I was still touching base with my clients, but there was really not a lot to be done. It was a break from my regular workaday world. The biggest struggle was giving myself the permission to completely surrender to the FREEDOM.

It was a practice in trust — letting go of responsibility and letting others lead the way and being completely open to whatever happens next, at least most of the time.

Strap on your seatbelt and join me for Mammoth May.

APRIL 29

I flew to Quito, Ecuador to join Anu, Bee, Lucy and Karen for a couple of nights, and a day to see a bit of the city on my own. A short walk from our apartment I was delighted to discover the largest neo-Gothic basilica in the Americas, the Basilica del Voto Nacional (Basilica of the National Vow — a reminder of Ecuador's Roman Catholic devotion to the Sacred Heart, Jesus' divine love for humanity.)

It was a treat to climb up inside the roof, across the entire length of the church ceiling and up the steeple on the other side. The rickety rope railings were certainly not up to code, which helped me exercise my COURAGE muscle.

Afterward I jumped in a cab to the TeleférıQo cable car up the side of the Pichincha Volcano to look out over Cruz Loma. It was a clear day down below, but the clouds consumed our swinging seats on the way up. There was no view at the top, just a misty mask, making for a very chilly wait in the long line going down.

That night we attempted to order a pizza, but our elusive Airbnb in the northeastern part of Old Town proved too difficult to find. Karen and Bee graciously offered to do a McDonalds drive-through in an Uber so that we could eat that night.

MAY 1

I flew to Galapagos Islands to grab the last few days of solo time. I'm used to traveling alone, so it was going to be interesting to see how I handle all this togetherness over the next month. I stayed at the Galapagos Dreams hotel in Puerto Ayora on Santa Cruz, the main island where the cruises start and home to the Darwin Center.

I discovered the little town, including the local markets and walked to the stunningly remote Galapagos Beach at Tortuga Bay. Then I took the water taxi back to town to do an afternoon snorkel trip around Academy Bay. Then I got up enough COURAGE to book my scuba dive for the next day.

The dive in the channel between Isla Baltra and Isla Santa Cruz was turbulent and turbid, with little to show for it. Though the dive was disappointing, I learned a very important lesson. This may be more relevant at the equator but it's something to consider regardless. Only book dives close to the new moon, as the full moon apparently draws the sediment up from the bottom of the ocean, decreasing visibility dramatically. You learn something new every day.

Back at the hotel, I did manage to get some work done before losing internet connection on the boat for the rest of the week!!

MAY 4-9

At noon the next day, I joined the cruise gang at the Darwin Centre and tried to help poor Svetlana adjust to the island life after her horrible travel connections. After a few drinks we were ready to board the Nemo I for five glorious days at sea, where we only saw one other boat the entire time.

Cruising the islands was spectacular and worth every penny. We were treated to snorkeling escapades with penguins and sea lions, giant turtles and sharks, and even attempted to swim with a school of dolphins. They proved to be a little too quick for us. The endless display of marine life was jaw dropping. The hundreds of boobies, black iguanas and giant land tortoises were just a few of the highlights, but it was the baby sea lion we watch for an hour that made us all fall in love.

It was sad to leave those islands but leave me must, filled with a new knowledge and appreciation for the magic they hold. We bade farewell to the motley crew and El Capitan (who offered to be my future husband if I ever decided to settle in Santa Cruz). Galapagos Islands were another bucket list item checked — but still on the list for a revisit.

MAY 9 TO 10

I only scheduled one day and night in Guayaquil, in hindsight probably deserving of more time but not on this trip. Svetlana had to work, so I took some time to unwind before we had the driver pick us up for a little tour before heading to the airport. I managed to climb the 445 stairs up to the lighthouse on top of Las Peñas in Cerro Santa Ana. If it weren't for our driver taking a break to DJ at the restaurant we stopped at for lunch, we would have made it to the airport on time. Dang!

We finally found another flight to take us to Lima in time to catch our connecting flight to Cusco the next morning. Staying at the Lima airport hotel was a little more expensive but it's the only way to go.

MAY 11 TO 15

This crazy Amazon adventure was a fabulous filler between Galapagos and Machu Picchu — a what-the-heck-while-you're-there-you-might-as-well-do-it type of trip from Cusco. Svetlana was game, and Shruti and Melissa joined us from Lima. This epic exploit had its apocalyptic moments though. The 16-hour drive from Cusco took us into the cloud forest, through the little town of Paucartambo, known for its annual Virgen Del Carmen festival where traditional dancers from all around compete for regional prizes. Then on we went, deeper into the Amazon along a single lane road carved into the side of the steep and treacherous mountains.

We stopped for lunch on the side of the road and watched the woolly monkeys have a threesome in the tree high above us. Welcome to the Amazon! Our driver had a sixth sense for spotting birds while he navigated the winding narrow rubble of a road, so we got close up to a Cock-of-the-Rock, Peru's national bird, and dozens more colourful species along the way.

It was after dark by the time we arrived at the lodge just outside of Shintuya on the edge of the Manu Reserve. Well not quite at the lodge. The river took away the road, so first we had to trudge 500 meters through the pitch dark forest with flashlights along a makeshift path in ankle-deep muck. I almost lost my boots (and my composure) coming very close to falling flat on my face. I recovered, but it was not one of my more graceful maneuvers. Good thing it was dark. That was just Day One – perhaps an auspicious sign of things to come.

Day Two took us downriver in two stages — one with a larger boat, the second with a much smaller boat to navigate the Rio Madre de Dios, one of the tributaries of the great Amazon river that flows down from Brazil. The river was just like you see on Planet Earth — alive with creatures including a white caiman resting on the shore. I was grateful for our sturdy boat and experienced captain.

Our destination that afternoon was a work-in-progress camp, out in the middle of freaking nowhere. Hot and sweaty from a day traveling in the jungle, I was relieved to lie down in the river and wash my hair. The pleasure lasted only for the moment. Then another discomfort would surface. When I emerged from the rushing water, the mosquitoes had already sent out the call, "Fresh meat! Let's eat!"

By the time I made it back to the cabin, the swarms had eaten their fill and I was covered in what would become itchy, raging water-filled blisters by bedtime. The cabins on stilts swayed with every step and their bathrooms where nowhere close to finished — merely a hole in the floor where the toilet would some day perch.

I managed to craft a funnel in case nature called in the middle of the night, as the stairs up to the tree house had no railings. Even if they did, I wasn't about to traipse across the muddy land to the 'open concept' toilet, sheltered only by the darkness, to invite even more hungry appetites.

We survived the evening, forfeiting the night walking tour for the relative safety of our mosquito net shrouded beds. But none of us were happy campers. The 100% deet that ate through Shruti's plastic shoes, and who knows what else, did little to curb those little critters' appetites. I stayed up most of the night scratching, stabbing and dousing with AfterBite — nothing seemed to work — until I eventually drifted off exasperated.

Daybreak came early, thank God! I was grateful for the funnel. After a somber breakfast during which tensions were high, we were invited on the tour's signature "jungle walk". It was met with some resistance. I think we were all pretty done with the jungle at that point but it was better than being sitting ducks for further insect attacks, and turned out to be quite a fascinating experience. When you least expect it, HAPPINESS can prevail.

After lunch we were instructed to prepare for our floating tube expedition — this was the clincher that sold me on this particular tour. Admittedly the price was good too, so we couldn't complain too much about the accommodations.

With our gear packed in the boat and swimsuits on, we launched our giant inner tubes down the lazy river. Tentative at first, then growing more relaxed as we maneuvered our inflated crafts together and apart, like synchronized swimmers along the way. Being carried downstream was intoxicating. The FREEDOM of floating put us all in a buoyant mood – and soothed my enraged mosquito bites.

Before we knew it the rapids were approaching. What was it he said we should do at the rapids? I desperately searched for our guide for some reminder — maybe a hand signal indicating what to do. I spotted him, but nothing. Just a smile and a wave — like, "Nice knowing you."

Hang on and hope to hell you make it to the other side. Yeah, I think that was it. Feet forward, I braced myself as we picked up speed — my heart was racing. Another breakthrough of COURAGE was about to hit.

Ahead of me was Svetlana — I watched helplessly as the water picked up the front of her tube and flipped her over backwards like a fried egg on a skillet, her pale pink legs making the perfect V-shape before disappearing over her head.

It was the same shape my legs made as the water started to push my tube up, obliterating my view. So mesmerized by Svetlana's unfortuitous dismount, I didn't realize I was headed for the same destiny. I straightened my legs and forced down the front of the tube just in time. That's what he said to do at the rapids!

I cleared the turbulence and jumped into rescue mode. Poor Svetlana was bobbing like a drunken cork, desperately grasping for help. Good thing we had life vests! Melissa and I swooped in to hold her up with the intention of taking her downstream to the gentle banks waiting ahead. To our shock, she broke away and foolishly attempted to hang on to a fallen tree.

Like a giant vacuum, the water sucked her under. With the last of her strength, she scrambled onto the trunk, which broke under her weight, almost sending her back into the river. The entire ordeal took only seconds, but the suffering lasted for the rest of the day.

Frazzled, Svetlana refused to get back on the inner tube, thinking the boat would be a safer alternative. "Fresh meat! Let's eat!", I could here the battle cry over the rushing water as the shadow of mosquitoes swarmed her boat. Then I turned my attention back to the river. This was the best part of the trip — although no one dared share that with Svetlana.

The rest of the day was making our way to our final camp (or so we thought), which was thankfully the best of them all, situated on the river where we had changed boats on the way in. It was beside the village where our guide grew up — so a homecoming of sorts. It was Mothers Day weekend and mama was happy to have her son home for a hug.

After the dust settled for the tourists, we were fed and put to bed, very ready to head back to Cusco in the morning. From my cozy cot, the rain's soothing sound lulled me to sleep. Throughout the night a rampage of thunderstorms passed through. In my ignorance, I enjoyed them. But our guide was not so impressed, knowing what would befall us in the morning.

High rivers mean danger, with debris being dragged off the shores and aimed straight at boat captains daring or stupid enough to navigate the torrential currents. Our destination was upstream, with only enough fuel to get us there on a relatively calm day. This was not what any of us could have imagined. We were to stay put until the captain gave us the all clear.

By noon, it was deemed safe enough, alhough once out on the river, I wondered if it's safe any day. White knuckled and eager landlubbers, we patiently sat while the captain revved the outboard motor up stream through the oncoming ebbs and flows of the Amazon River, eventually bringing us back to dry land near the little town of Pillcopata.

Off to a late start and with that 11-hour drive still ahead of us, we packed up the van with some added hitchers from the village. The road revealed the true damage caused by the rain. There were people walking down the road in the middle of nowhere. Where did they come from? Where are they going? They brought with them the bad news that a landslide had blocked the road and road crews had not yet arrived. After all, it was Mothers Day.

We were given a choice: stick with the program and potentially get stuck on the road overnight, or turn back to find safe haven for the night, then start off again early the next morning. We took a vote — the safe haven won. So I spent Mothers Day in a lovely (by jungle standards) cabin in the Amazon jungle desperately trying to get a signal on Svetlana's phone to call home.

Although I could have gone either way on the vote, I was glad we did not try to navigate that road in the dark. The daylight drive was terrifying enough. Happy to arrive back to Cusco, I immediately got cleaned up, licked my wounds and tucked myself under the covers with a nice cup of coca tea — ravenous for some decent internet connection after four harrowing days in the jungle.

MAY 16-17

A good night's sleep can do you a world of good — if you have enough oxygen. Altitude sickness is very real. It's what happens when your blood thickens, making it harder for your heart to pump oxygen to all your body parts.

I woke up gasping for air. It was freaky. Some deep breathing exercises, loads of water and coca tea, gave me just enough energy to get me moving and join the walking tour that morning. I never thought of a walking tour as a survival technique, but I was certain if I stayed in bed I would have suffocated.

My friends arrived that morning, and thankfully Michael and Brian were up and ready to go on the walk. We left Rada and Pauline to rest and took off to find the walking tour location.

Cusco is the gateway to Machu Picchu. It was the administrative, political and military centre of Incan civilization from the early 13th century. The Incan Empire dominated the west coast of South America from Ecuador to Santiago, Chile until the Spanish took over in 1572 and buried all Incan places of worship under their Roman Catholic churches. The Incan culture is so strongly embedded in today's Cusco that even the Catholic priests show up for the Incan nature-based rituals, like summer and winter solstice celebrations and other offerings to the earth. It's a fascinating place, worth spending more time to explore.

We had a day to get it all in before heading off to Machu Picchu. It was great to hang with my peeps again — people my age, people from home, people I can relate to effortlessly.

What a sweet treat during this month of madness, this year of expanding opportunities. It was nice to be touched by home, even just for a little while.

MAY 17-19

Early the next day we were off on our Inca Trail trek with Alpaca Expeditions, which for various reasons was reduced to one day. At the Ollantaytambo train station, we boarded the train toward Aguas Caliente. An hour or so in, Pauline and Shruti, Michael and Brian, and I were dropped off at the side of the train tracks directly below the Wiñay Wayna ruins, while the others continued on the train to Aguas Caliente. The trek started with a 600-meter vertical ascent up the switchback porters' trail. Every painstaking, sweat-soaked, lung-burning minute of it brought me more HAPPINESS. I was finally free from the limitations that have held me back from doing the one thing I've always wanted to do in my life.

The view at the top was spectacular. Looking down the steep slope of the Wiñay Wayna ruins made me wonder what it was like back in the day. Lunch at the base camp was delicious and well deserved. We were off on the trail again for a more few hours, eventually climbing the monkey steps before emerging through the Sun Gate.

If my life were to end in the moment I stood in front of Machu Picchu, I would have been happy. The spiritual nature of that site would have lifted my soul straight to heaven. It was everything I wanted it to be and more.

Arriving so late in the day gave us the feeling that we owned the place. The only problem was that we had to leave so soon.

I wanted to stay — find a place to lie and absorb the richness of the land, sleep in the arms of spirit in the holy palace of the ancient Incas. So many years I've waited for this moment. I wanted to cherish it, capture it and put it in a time capsule so that I can bathe in its beauty for eternity.

"The last bus is leaving!" The message from our trusty guide fell like ancient Incan stones on my ears. Seriously? I surrendered my fantasy and resigned myself to the inevitable, content in knowing I would be back up again by bus the next morning. I headed toward the exit, but not before Shruti and I had a close encounter with an alpaca or two — it's just so Machu Picchu up here.

Although it was still spectacular in every way, for some reason I didn't connect as much to the place the next day. It could have been the crowds, it could have been the added dynamics of the group or it could have been the bus and the lack of sweat to get there. Whatever was missing, I savoured the day but still I'm not ready to take this one off the list yet either. I would love to return one day with the love of my life. Better get busy on that when I get home.

MAY 19-24

After a couple of fabulous nights in Aguas Caliente, I parted ways with my Remote pals and followed my Canadian peeps back to Cusco, then on to Lima where we met friend's of Rada, Luchio (a Lima native living in Toronto) and Gavin (a surprise small world connection from a completely different group of friends back home.) They decided to join us in Lima to enhance our city experience. After a few days of indulging in fine wines, fabulous foods and a little touring around, I had to say farewell to my Canadian friends. Lima is lovely, but I had to leave the lap of luxury and head off into Bolivian Oblivion.

MAY 25-31

It was time for Nathan's Excellent Adventure, a full five-day Bolivian tour of Lake Titicaca, La Paz and the famous Uyuni Salt Flats, starting with a celebratory tasting menu and wine pairing hosted by Nathan (he really is a classy guy) at one of the best restaurants in La Paz.

This was followed by non-stop escapades that started with a bus ride to Lake Titicaca. After lunch in Copacabana we got onboard a little boat and headed to Isla del Sol (Island of the Sun) to climb the Escalera del Inca and drink from the fountain of youth. The island claims to be the birthplace of the first Incas, with feminine and masculine iconic references decorating its shores. There were ruins to be discovered there, but we didn't have time to dally.

Back on the boat we went, to visit a touristy, non-occupied version of Puno's famous floating islands, then back to Copacabana for a stay at a cold hotel. Oh right, I forgot to tell you, we were back to chasing winter again. May in South America is like November in North America.

The next morning we were on the bus again back to La Paz.

That bus took us around La Paz, where we got a fabulous panoramic view from Killi Killi lookout and then on to the bus station for dinner and the overnight bus to Uyuni. There we stayed at a very cool hostel before heading to the Great Train Graveyard and the Tiawanaku ruins in our convoy of six rough and rugged jeeps. I shared with Brian, Gianni, Mikko, Todd and his lovely fiancée Rebecca — the romance emerged after meeting back in Mexico City. Just one of the many successful remote romances! I'm happy to say I'll be attending their wedding on the west coast next summer.

The train graveyard was enchanting. Heavy eroding steam-engines sinking into piles of wind-swept salty sand. Standing there it was hard to believe that the site was once the main junction of train transport to the coast for the mining industry. Gems like these are only uncovered when you travel off the beaten track.

It was time to head out into the world's largest salt flats, or Salar, for a couple of days. There's over 10,000 square kilometers or 4,000 sqare miles of salt, at an elevation of

3600 meters or 12,000 feet above sea level. It's so flat and white that it's used for satellite calibrations. It's so big we only crossed a tiny little wedge at the bottom.

Incahuasi, the coral island in the middle of the Salar, tells of the giant prehistoric lake Minchin that used to cover the area. It's believed at one point in history that the entire area was under the sea – thus the salt.

A long, flat drive and a homemade lunch welcomed us to the Palacio de Sal hotel (one of the stops on the DAKAR world rally competition that goes from Lima, Peru to Cordoba, Argentina) built with — you guessed it — salt blocks. We ended our journey at the not-so-fancy hostel we affectionately called the Ice Prison.

The next day a long drive took us past mountains and lake that were home to Andean flamingos, so unexpected after my sightings in Galapagos. A snowy mountain pass sent us on a detour to a makeshift accommodation for the night — a simple series of rooms all crammed full of beds where we were to all sleep together.

That was just too much togetherness for me. This was my tipping point. I completely lost it and had a meltdown. It was an epic journey and I was so grateful to be part of it, but after a month on the move, landing in Bolivian Oblivion sent me into a tailspin — a temporary lapse in stoicism — with nothing to catch my fall. I'm pretty sure I cried myself to sleep that night.

Next day's bus and our flight to Cordoba couldn't come fast enough. I am glad, though, that I was part of a smaller group that ventured farther south to check out the phenomenal rock formations near Alota and enjoyed another lunch freshly made by our drivers in the little town of Mallku Villa Maria, at the bottom tip of our route. Then there was the long drive back up to Uyuni to freshen up for dinner and prepare for the overnight bus back to La Paz.

I was ready to go. I was done, finished, spent.

I'm exhausted just writing this. I can't believe I actually did all that. Now, of course, I have another Life Hack for you.

Self Care Hack

This type of travel takes endurance and a lot of self-care. Keeping active on the road is important, especially when you spend so much time sitting in airports, planes, buses and cars.

Equally important is caring for your self emotionally. It's important to nurture your feelings — be accepting of what comes up in moments of stress, fear or anger. Find time every day to be still and meditate. Simply focus on the breath and pay attention as thoughts emerge. Say "thank you" to your thoughts and go back to the breath.

Take a little extra time each day just to stretch or do some yoga. If you prefer to follow instruction, I found free videos on YouTube called Yoga with Adriene.

There are tons of little things you can do every day to take good care of yourself on the road or at home. Check out Author's Resource section for tips from Bri, our Ikigai fitness coach and hairdresser extraordinaire.

WRAPPING UP AN AMAZING MONTH

Traveling with a group, large or small, has its perks and its challenges. I am someone who truly appreciates my quiet time alone. So as much as I love my fellow Remotes and my friends from back home, I'm forced to agree with my Dad, that it's just too much togetherness. I held it together by finding mini-escapes to get away from the maddening crowd.

Other than that Bolivian breakdown, the month unfolded perfectly. It really was an Excellent Adventure. Thanks Nathan.

How does one end a month like that? With a friend like Michael M. or Bee or anyone that has the pass — the Priority Pass for airport lounges, that is. I was blessed to be the guest on a few occasions, but I think this one was the most appreciated.

After the overnight bus from Uyuni dropped us off at the back entrance to the La Paz airport at five in the morning, we dragged our luggage for a kilometer before checking in. After a short flight from La Paz, the lounge in the Santiago, Chile airport between our connection to Cordoba was like heaven. It was fun to run into a couple of Remote Year executives in the lounge. That's what happens when you are part of a large and growing community.

Travel Hack

Relaxing in an airport lounge before or between flights can make a world of difference in a long travel day. Some higher priced flights will include access, but assuming you are traveling economy, then get yourself a Priority Pass through Amex, or check your bank credit card benefits. At US $35-50 per visit, paying the extra fee might be worth it if you plan to do a lot of travel. Some credit cards, like the Chase Sapphire, allow unlimited guests, so you could quickly become the most popular person in your group.

Month 11: Nose to the Grindstone

Destination: Argentina – Cordoba ~ June

The gaucho is the wild and nomadic, brave and unruly skilled horseman of the Argentine plains. Sounds a little like Remotes except for the skilled horseman part. Giddy up! Time to get back to work and make some money to pay for this endless adventure. But while you're at it, you might as well get back up on that horse again and live the gaucho life.

It was time to move on to the final country on our grand adventure — Argentina, way on the other side of South America. Farewell to the Incas, a tearful goodbye to decent coffee and dark chocolate, and good riddance to the endless touring.

That insane month of travel had to come to an end. I couldn't afford to keep living that type of lifestyle — financially, physically or emotionally. It's exhausting. But it is truly tough to balance the responsibilities of running a business with the temptations of travel.

It was time to put my head down and get back to work. It was also nice to get back to a regular meal schedule — farmers markets, fresh produce and home-cooked meals. There's that strange sense of FREEDOM again — the type of FREEDOM that gives you wiggle room when you are grounded in a regular schedule.

SETTLING INTO ARGENTINA

Cordoba is a university town with none of the typical touristy things to do or see. The temptations would be fewer, so I could focus on my work and getting back to those Spanish lessons. I signed up for lessons at the Set Idiomas, close to the co-working space, with Betsy, Erica and Michael. I discovered, however, that Argentine Spanish is very different, kind of like an Italian version, which made it even harder to learn. So confusing. I'll just have to stick with the Mexican version of Spanish.

La Maquinita Coworking space in Cordoba was great, with a fun local working community. Most of the Ikigais who frequented the workspace had full time jobs with employers or teams to report to. Some just preferred to be in the company of others while working. There were always employees of Remote Year popping in and out over the course of the year, which made it even more dynamic.

By the time we arrived in Cordoba we were down to 55 people. The rest had gone home for various reasons or split off from the group to travel on their own. Those that remained worked in jobs like Jason, the sales and travel designer, and Kara, the real estate broker, and Samvita, the health certification consultant.

There were all types of digital programming folks like Bee, Ben, Gerry, Jordan, JP, Kash, Magic, Maijid, Marko, Morgan and Devin. Then there were a variety of marketing functions held by Ariel, Betsy, Laura, Mai and Hilary W.

There were freelance copywriters like Brian and Lauren, designers like Erica and Jen, as well as project managers like Michael M., Bambi, Gina and Janesse. Stacy and Karen are accountants, while Taylor worked as a headhunter, and Todd was grading nursing papers online.

There was a financial analyst, UX designers, a brain scientist, an operations manager and a construction estimator. There were matchmakers, travel writers and a whole host of business owners like Ankur, Hilary B, Nathan and Svetlana.

There are as many job functions or freelance skills as there are people in the digital nomad world. So just decide what you are good at and take it on the road. If you need a little extra COURAGE to convince your employer to let you do this, have a chat with Dan. He's created a whole program to help people turn their office-based jobs remote. Check out the Authors Resources in the back of the book to see who's doing what now.

NOW GET TO WORK!

It might be easier to get your work done if you have an employer or team to report to or project deadlines to follow. The life of a digital nomad is full of FREEDOM, but being your own boss requires a lot of discipline. When you run your own show, staying focused on new business development is hard at the best of times, never mind when the choice is between tracking down new leads and visiting the Galapagos Islands! There is just no contest.

Business Hack

Keep in mind that at least 10% of your productive time should be spent on new business development. That could be anything from networking to following up on leads. It takes a lot of COURAGE to put yourself out there and risk rejection.

The sales call is the most important piece of the funnel. If you can't close, you won't have any business. The most successful entrepreneurs have the same personality profile as high-performing sales people. There is a lot to learn in overcoming objections and holding the tension between a prospect's current state and their desired future state. I think all entrepreneurs, startups and freelancers should have sales training. I know it sounds like a dirty word but it could be the difference between success and failure.

If you are selling online products, your sales page or video sales letter is key. It must follow the best practices of direct sales and take the prospect along the path to purchase without any human interaction. Rather than spending time doing it yourself, hire an expert copywriter, like Brian, he's the direct marketing copywriting king.

BUSINESS IS CONSTANTLY EVOLVING

Fortunately I have some very loyal clients who stuck with me throughout the year, and I had the opportunity to work with some of my fellow Remotes to build their businesses. The rental income from my house was what kept me above water.

However, there was another personal project I had wanted to work on since before this year started, and this felt like the right time to launch. I had purchased a domain called NiceLife.ca back in November. I felt there was something I could do with it over time, and now was the time to get it done. With only two months left on our itinerary and a very real urge to ground myself in Cordoba, there was no excuse to put it off any longer.

Being a strategic creative marketing expert, I've developed many businesses, products, brands, and websites over the years. So I knew the task of creating the NiceLife.ca site with all its integrations would take a lot of time.

My original intention was to create a blogging site where I could share tips about business, travel, relationships and life in general. When I surveyed the folks on my list, they told me that they felt the most important thing to have in order to lead a nice life was HAPPINESS.

So I decided to focus on happiness as a starting point for my content. I wrote blogs about happiness, researched happiness and practiced bringing more happiness into my life every day. But being a businessperson, I also wanted to make some money at this.

Creating digital products to sell online, along with building the marketing tactics, follow-up strategies and sales conversion can be a recipe for brain drain and ultimate burnout. I know from experience, there had to be a better way. A fellow Remote, Taylor told me about a physical product online business model that I wanted to try.

In order to launch the website I had to sell something! People told me they wanted Happiness — so I started to sell Happiness. That's right — Happy T-shirts, Happy necklaces, whatever happy thing I could find. The business of selling physical products with bonuses online was fascinating to me, but I needed to educate myself in this physical product business model. I purchased the program Taylor recommended with step-by-step instructions and loads of support.

I made the commitment to chip away at the website every day. With any start-up it always takes longer than you think, and some days it feels like pushing a boulder up a hill. But perseverance is the key. As any successful entrepreneur knows — no pain, no gain. Failure is only a sign that you are getting closer to success. I spent the month laying down a foundation that I hope will be an ongoing revenue stream for my retirement. Retirement? Who am I kidding?!

Business Hack

There is no such thing as residual income without working at it. Don't buy anyone's BS about making six figures without putting in the time. Every business takes time, money and effort to build. Sure, you can learn from others who have done it before you. Absolutely, you can avoid mistakes by listening to self-proclaimed "gurus". But at the end of the day, you still need to do the work. That is why 80% of startups fail — because people think it's easy. They imagine some kind of ultimate FREEDOM when in fact running your own successful business doesn't ever stop. You may be freed from the cubicle or the nine-to-five time slot, but be prepared to work even longer hours. The burdens of accounting, operations, sales and marketing can be much heavier. But once you are up and running, the rewards are greater.

Even though they may be self-imposed, there is no denying the importance of deadlines. If it weren't for my commitment to launch this book by a specific time, you would not be reading it now. There would have been a million other things that could have diverted my attention. I believe the tighter the deadline the better. It causes something called, "Creative Tension", a healthy anxiety that forces creative problem solving and productivity. If you are inspired to achieve anything in business or life, give it a seriously short deadline. Then find an accountability partner to keep your feet to the fire. You'll be amazed at what you can get done in a day, a week or a month.

ALL WORK AND NO PLAY

I'm the type of person who is all in or all out. I know it's important to take breaks, but when I'm in the flow it's hard to break away. My work style tends to be intense while I'm working, but when I'm done, I'm done. Although Cordoba isn't an enticing city with a lot of new shiny objects to distract the easily sidetracked entrepreneur, it does offer a host of interesting and educational experiences about Argentina and its history.

The free walking tours were incredible, the Muy Güemes neighbourhood was delightful and with our awesome Experience Lead, Coti, at the helm, the month was dotted with truly authentic local track events.

It all started on the first weekend, with our visit to the Monkey Rehabilitation Center, about two hours outside Cordoba near La Cumbre. Here, over 150 monkeys have been rescued from domesticated and/or abusive situations and repatriated back to nature.

Maria Alejandra founded the center over 20 years ago, when a large parcel of land was donated to the cause. She runs the place with keen focus on the animals — we heard that the monkeys eat better than the volunteers do. We spent the day touring the grounds and delivering food to groups of monkeys at each stage of their rehabilitation. It was a fascinating process, and to see the hard work and commitment by their team was humbling.

One of the Remote Year groups that visited before us had made it their Positive Impact project to build a better online presence and a more sustainable business model, and we were able to help. The monkeys still need your help. If you are interested, you can check out the center here at caraya.org.

LIVING THE GAUCHO LIFE

Another day in the country had me back up on a horse living the Gaucho Life, although I was nervous about saddling up again after my last experience in Colombia. Like most animals, horses have an uncanny sense of energy, and they know when their rider is in control. Luckily I was much more in control this time.

I mounted my golden mare with confidence and enjoyed every minute of our ride out on the Pampa — the fertile plains of the region. I appreciated the steadiness with which she navigated the stony slopes, was grateful for her response to my lead and laughed at her constant calls to the wild horses that roamed the area. I would love to know what she was saying.

Our traditional asado at the corral was complete with ribs, beef and sausage, and the best empanadas I've ever tasted. We were able to groom the horses and watch the gauchos replacing the horseshoes. This close up and personal experience grounded me back on the earth once again.

Back in the city, there was some musical inspiration waiting for us the next week. One evening we visited a traditional artisan, Mariano Paz, who shared the secrets of one of Argentina's most historic trades, Bombo drum making. After seeing the intricate, time consuming process, we all had an opportunity to discover how music and friends were made in pre-colonial times.

The following weekend we visited a unique communal home called Cabezas de Tormenta, where designers, artists, chefs, musicians and performers collaborate on innovative projects to entertain guests at invitation-only events. This was something the tourists don't experience.

Our experience leaders continued to exceed our expectations with events like the Green Cocktail at Apartamento bar in Muy Güemes, right across from the weekend art fair. The passionate bartender influenced by her Grandma's ancient healing remedies and herbal experimentation taught us the fine art of cocktail creation.

We spent an evening with a fun and interactive session with renowned photographer-cum-industrial designer Pablo Escribano, who uses recycled plastic to create fascinating light installations.

It was another inspiring month of engaging activities.

LIVE LIKE A LOCAL

As I've said before, the key to getting the most out of any travel adventure is to connect with locals. Some of the coolest track events gave us the opportunity to dine with a local family. Back in Mexico City, for example, we visited with Maria and her two adult children one evening. We helped prepare a traditional dinner and learned more about their lives. In Cordoba, Coti arranged for us to make empanadas with a local family.

These experiences help ground you when you're traveling. It was a great opportunity for them to learn about our adventures and life abroad, and there's nothing like a little home cooking to warm your heart.

Travel Hack
They say the experiences that create the most HAPPINESS in life happen when we have deep, meaningful connections with other people. The demand for this is influencing the travel business, with more travelers looking to connect with locals. Don't forget the DYI version of this exists already through Couchsurfers.com and various MeetUp type groups.

ARGENTINA'S DARK PAST

What was most fascinating to me in Cordoda was to learn more about Argentina's history. I had no idea that their famous past president, Juan Peron, was in cahoots with the Nazis, or the theories suggesting that Hilter actually escaped into the mountains of Patagonia. It made sense when you consider they were both mentored by Mussolini, and with the influx of German refugees into Argentina before, during and after WWII, it seemed to be a plausible conclusion.

I mentioned before that I was so over anything to do with the war because of my Dad's obsession with watching war footage on TV. I didn't think I would ever seek out more details of this outrageous time. While those small European towns saw the ravages of war, it's hard to believe that a country so far away would harbour these war criminals.

There is a little pedestrian-only town up in the hills outside Cordoba called La Cumbrasita. If you visit there, you feel you could be in Germany. It's a charming place with hilly streets, one of which leads to a waterfall hike. I went twice. (I did say there wasn't much to do in Cordoba.) One of those times was with Lee, Nandita and Ankur. They rented a car, so we stopped in the town of Alta Gracia, home to a fabulous monastery and Che Guevara's childhood home and museum.

ARGENTINA'S EVEN DARKER PAST

Argentina's more recent history is even more disturbing than its affiliations with Nazi Germany, although the atrocities are just as horrific. Between 1967 and 1983, over 30,000 people mysteriously disappeared (their remains never to be found) all because of their political leanings.

It was the movie *"Noche de los Lápices"* that showed us the warped thinking that literally killed the communist uprising. In an attempt to curb Russia's influence in an already socialist South America, the USA installed dictators to rule Argentina with an iron fist. No tolerance for student protests, no liberties for the working class, no rights for individual freedom of speech.

Argentina was a police state, and if you didn't obey the law you disappeared in the middle of the night along with anyone else you associated with. People of all ages were held in death camps, tried in secret courts at the whim of a capitalist-controlled military dictatorship. Sound familiar?

It was genocide of epic proportions, with human indignities likened to the horrors of Nazi Germany. Many children were born and adopted by regime-approved parents, many of those families from the military. They were never to be seen again.

To this day, the grandmothers of those victims, called the Abuelas of Plaza de Mayo, still hold vigil, wearing white head scarves, in main squares around Argentina every Thursday. They still hold out the hope that curious children of those lost will come forward to take a DNA test and reconnect to their real families.

October 2017 marked their 40th anniversary, with only 124 of an estimated 500 children being united with their biological families. The Abuelas' fight continues.

A BITTERSWEET CELEBRATION

One the more moving experiences I had in Cordoba was working with Marcos and Debora, partners in the Colectivo Manifiesto photojournalists' collective, to create a photo essay of the day when many of those responsible for Argentina's dark past were brought to justice — 40 years later. We worked with their photo-journalistic images to tell the story of that day of justice. It was an intimate exercise to see the faces of those who lived through it and finally attained some closure.

MEMOIRES OF TIME

For a "quiet" month, it certainly had its highlights, one of which was the hard work of our yearbook committee. Ikigai is so blessed to have such talented and energetic people committed to capturing our entire year for eternity. I'm so excited that tomorrow I will open my yearbook, which is lovingly wrapped under my Christmas tree.

I cherish the memories even more now than when they actually happened. Writing and editing this book has allowed me to live through the year again and again. I hope it's also a reminder to others who took the journey with me.

Legacy Hack

Take the time to capture your experiences for posterity. Life is not just about Instagram, Facebook and the compilation videos set to electronic music. Time-capsule your thoughts, your feelings and the wisdom you gained from it all. It doesn't have to be a traditional book or blog, but it does have to capture stories.

Stories are the heart of your experience. A good story has a beginning, a middle and an end. It has a conflict or a challenge you have to overcome. The best stories get people emotionally involved and teach a lesson or two in the process. You never know where your stories will take you.

Photo: Erica Brooks

Month 12: Dead of Winter at 25°C

Destination: Argentina – Buenos Aires ~ July

The weather was not hard to take in this grand dame of a city filled with a mish mash of architectural styles reflecting the of waves of European immigrants. Blink your eyes and you're in Paris. Blink again, you're in Madrid. Blink again, you're in London, New York or back in Buenos Aires. A great place to stay — too bad about the coffee.

It was July 1st, Canada Day, when we loaded up onto two buses in Cordoba for our last group transition of the year — one bus for the drunken drive and the other for those leaning less to libation.

Out of my suitcase came the Canadian flags I had been carrying all year just for this day. We played Canadian trivia. Karen and I (the only two Canadians on board) sang "Oh Canada" in a concerted effort to celebrate our country's 150th year.

I'll be coming home soon, but first I need to discover the last but not least fascinating city on our itinerary, Buenos Aires!

BUENAS NOCHES

July is the middle of winter in South America, so night falls early. By the time we arrived, it was dark, and the nightlife had not yet begun in the city that never sleeps. BA is truly the city that never stops, as I would later observe on a few sleepless nights at 4am on the balcony of my boutique hotel room in Palermo.

Palermo, like most of the barrios (neighbourhoods) that make up the city center, is alive with little shops, bars, cafes and restaurants offering up international and local cuisine — an endless choice of empanadas (savoury pastries), alfajores (dulce de leche filled cookies) and asados (Argentine BBQs).

One of the best asado restaurants (known as parillas) was located directly under my balcony, tempting me with smokey fumes every night to come have a taste. I did, of course, and the steak was excellent.

The city is wonderful and the BA government has done a great job of keeping it clean, relatively safe and tourist friendly.

Travel Hack

There are many options for walking tours, bike tours and bus tours, although I heard the Hop-On-Hop-Off bus was not so great, so I didn't bother trying it out. The city's official tourism website is an excellent source of info and the city-run free walking tours really are free (no tipping allowed).

Start making your plans here: turismo.buenosaires.gob.ar/en. These tours are okay for a basic understanding of the city, but you may find the not-so-free walking tours a more robust experience. As always, you get what you pay for.

Whatever you decide, if Buenos Aires is on your list, make sure you give it enough time. There is so much to see and do. There are also several expat communities you can connect with if you plan to stay a little longer.

It's really easy to get around. The transit system is super simple to navigate and very efficient if you have the COURAGE to give it a go. Although I preferred the Subte (underground) to the speed demon bus drivers on the surface, there are limits to where the subway can take you. But you can always walk from the station to wherever you want to go. Either way, buy a SUBE transit card and you are on your way to experiencing an incredible city.

Buenos Aires was waiting to entertain us with loads of cool stuff to do — starting with a Monday night Bomba concert, lots of wine tastings, tango shows, a food truck festival, the 127th annual Rural Exhibition, amazing museums, the Fuerza Bruta (coolest interactive show ever!), bike tours, graffiti tours, historical tours, private group session with shoemaking artist Josefina, a day-long goodbye party followed by farewell dinners every night of our last week.

With so much to do it was hard to balance business with the alluring events of our last month together. But I'm the type of person who can only enjoy the FREEDOM when I'm satisfied that my work is done.

BACK TO BUSINESS IN BA

Nathan had organized a Seven-Day-Start-Up event for those Ikigais and gals who wanted to implement a business before heading off in different directions. So for one week at the same time every day, we had a group call to report what we had achieved. Each day required a decision to be made and some work to be done to bring us closer to the launch of our new businesses.

I had a head start with the launch of my NiceLife.ca website in Cordoba. My intention for the Seven-Day-Start-Up was to monetize the site by integrating ecommerce and finding a physical product to sell. Using the knowledge and done-for-you products I gained from that online course I signed up for last month, I was able to follow the step-by-step process to launch the product on the website. The seven-day deadline sure put the pressure on, but as a result, I made my first sale before the end of the year.

Like all things in life, we don't deliver what is expected; we deliver what is inspected. The Seven-Day-Start-Up held me accountable, motivating me to make something happen because I said I would.

Business Hack

Don't set yourself up for failure by repeating the most common habit in the world, procrastination. As Thomas Edison once said, "Success is 1% inspiration and 99% perspiration." It's the stick-to-it-iveness of the individual that makes a dream come true. There are a million-and-one excuses in the world, but not one of them can get in the way of a visionary. Don't wait until everything is perfect. Done is better than none.

Running an online business from abroad is tough, but if you have the right team and support systems in place, it can be a lot easier. It was a blessing to have a bunch of digital experts at hand in our group — it was like traveling with my own IT department!

If you are solo you can always find people through networking or the growing number of the online resource sites, like upwork.com or toptal.com or the competition-based site freelancers.com. There's fiverr.com, Guru.com, 99designs.com, peopleperhour.com and dozens more. You can even post freelance projects on Craigslist! Just make sure you are clear on what you want and know what to look for in a valuable and trustworthy resource.

Be prepared to deal with potential fraud alerts from your bank or surprise credit card cancellations if you are doing business abroad. Even though some banks don't require you to advise them of your travel plans, it's wise to do so. If you plan to make any large online purchases, then definitely call them ahead.

Make sure your wifi connection is secure. Using your mobile phone as a hot spot provides a more secure connection than any wifi that is shared with other users.

Consider setting up your business from home before venturing off. That way you can test all the integration and security, and validate the business model, before venturing off into the distractions of the world. Then, when you are abroad you'll be able to focus on your marketing and customer service.

I powered through so much work in the last few weeks of our year. When I wasn't holed up in my room attached to my computer, I tracked 10,000 steps a day around the city. I pushed myself so hard, I was hit hard with a cold. It sucked to miss the last weeks of bonding and bars, but I was content that I had done as much as I could do. But even with that raging head cold, I did force myself to attend our last supper!

The menu was an assortment of dishes from all the places we traveled over the year — a good idea that failed miserably in execution. But it wasn't about the food that night; it was about the circle.

Gianni and Claire had arranged for us to form a circle in the wine cellar of the restaurant before dinner. We went around the circle one-by-one, each of us lighting our candle and sharing what we learned, how we grew, what changed, what stayed the same. The friendships, the follies, the fantasy, and the fun!

I realized that I hadn't really changed very much over the year. I was content to have had the COURAGE, experienced the FREEDOM and called on HAPPINESS no matter where I went or what I did.

It was a powerful way for us to close the group by honoring each other's journey.

What's Next?

Destination: Canada –Toronto~August

It was the perfect time to return home. Everyone was in summer holiday mode, so there were lots of opportunities to reunite and reconnect. I was happy to be back where I understood the language and knew where everything was – familiar food, familiar faces, and familiar places.

I'm deeply grateful for the experiences and the people I met along this journey. I'm thrilled that I had the COURAGE to take a leap of faith and do this crazy thing. Would I do it again? Absolutely! Would I do it over? – probably not in the same way.

I will always be a traveler. South Africa calls me every October and I have no intention of hibernating every winter in the frozen north. The summer months are made for road trips. There is still a lot more of the world to see. As a Remote Year Citizen I can join any of the groups in any of the cities at any time - if there's room — so I will definitely be doing that sometime soon. They also have four-month programs. So there are lots of options.

These stories are told from my own perspective – that's all I know. We all experience life differently and now it's your turn. What have you been procrastinating on, putting off or shoving to the back burner for a 'better time'? There is no better time than now to make your dream a reality.

NOW DO SOMETHING ABOUT IT

If you made it this far then I assume you found something interesting, inspiring or moving about the stories, the people and the places we went to. Maybe one of the Life Hacks spoke to you. Perhaps you got a little taste of FREEDOM. Before you put down the book, take a few minutes to create your own version of the Nice Life.

WHAT? SO WHAT? NOW WHAT?

Here is a great game I learned at one of those creativity conferences. Get out a pen to jot down your thoughts. There may be a life-changing nugget revealed in your answers.

What? What stood out for you in this book? What do you remember vividly? What had special meaning or connection to your experience of life? What did you learn? What inspired you to think, feel or act in a different way?

There are no right answers. It only matters that it resonates with you. There may be several things, so look at them all separately. Now ask yourself the next question.

So What? Why is this thing important to you? What significance does it hold? What thoughts or feelings does it bring up and why? How can you relate to the situations or stories? What does it mean for you in your life now?

Now that you have investigated your *What?* and *So What?*, what are you going to do about it?

Now What? How you are going to use this new learning, insight or story? How will you do, think or feel differently as a result of this enquiry? What is going to be different in your life moving forward?

LET COURAGE GUIDE YOU

COURAGE is the ability to persevere — no matter what. If you want something bad enough, you will make it happen. Determination is the driving emotion that helps you overcome obstacles. It takes courage to keep moving forward. Face the fear and do it anyway.

Courage is about staying the course even when the stakes are high. Courage is doing your due diligence to ensure your safety. Courage is listening to your own inner guidance (not only the gremlin) and thwarting the negativity of others. Have courage in your commitment. You've got this.

TAKE THE TIME FOR YOU

It's time for you to find the COURAGE to take steps toward your own personal bucket list. Give yourself the permission to go for your own version of FREEDOM. Remember that HAPPINESS is not out there. It lives in the choices you make every day.

May your journey be smooth and your life full of joy.

See you out there!

WHAT?

_____
_____
_____
_____

SO WHAT?

_____
_____
_____
_____

NOW WHAT?

_____
_____
_____
_____
_____

Author's Resources

IKIGAIS AT WORK

Here's a shout out to some of the super-talented and highly-skilled Ikigais and gals I traveled with for a year. This is what they've been working on. Some new projects and some jobs that let them work remotely. Check out their links. It's a small world. You might know them, run into them or need their services sometime in the future.

Anu Vijayamohan – *Digital Douchebag* aims to bring some humor to the very serious "digital nomad posing with laptop" industry - check out the irony and sarcasm on Instagram **@digitaldouchebag** or **Facebook.com/digitaldouchebag**

Annie Kingston is a travel blogger and content writer. Born and raised in Kingston, Ontario, Canada, she now lives as a digital nomad and has been to 60 countries. You can follow her adventures at **www.catchmeifyoucannie.com**

Ariella Meranus and Jeff Hudson – *Talk Crypto To Me* is your go-to resource for blockchain, bitcoin, and all things crypto, explained simply. By making crypto simple, accessible, and funny/fun, their newsletter, website, e-book and podcast make it easy to be "in-the-know" on crypto. Check them out at **talkcryptotome.io**

Bharathi Balasubramanyam – Full stack developer with a weakness for chocolate and Harry Potter. See her portfolio at **www.beebha.com**

Bri Alvis – A fitness & health coach with easy-to-follow programs. Find her on **facebook.com/bri.alvis.7**

Brian McCarthy – A *Direct Response Copywriter* who helps businesses boost online sales. He works primarily in the personal development and "build your online business" markets, writing emails and sales pages that have earned 7-figures for his clients. He's also really good at Little Mermaid karaoke. You can stalk him at his website: **ThePDCopywriter.com**

Dan Mikail – Looking for a remote job? You might already have one. Our experts help clients successfully turn their office-based jobs remote. We'll guide you through every step of the process from building a business case to how to approach your boss and other stakeholders. Visit our website for course details and enrolment. We can't wait to help you ditch the desk. **remotejobcoach.com**

Erica Brooks – *Hello Creative Solutions* is a freelance business with an eye for design and a heart for telling a captivating story, Erica's expertise is robust content, including custom-published magazines, eBooks, white papers, infographics and annual reports. **hellocreativesolutions.com**

Jordan Klocko and Jeff Hansen – The one totally indispensable tool in the digital nomad's toolkit is WiFi – sadly it does not always meet the daily demands of remote workers. A better solution is on its way, sign up today! Launching soon at **nomadifi.me**

Kara Keets – Moving in? Moving out? Moving up? Navigate the world of real estate with experts you can trust. The team at *Texas Residents* will guide you HOME. **karakeetonrealestate.com**

Lee Wagner – A blogger, travel writer, and photographer. Check out the blog to follow her stories on the road. Lee is also available for travel writing! Download her FREE ebook, *"Travel the World for Next to Nothing"* at **bonanzaroad.com**

Maijid Moujaled – *Chipper Cash* is a mobile payments app targeted towards emerging markets. It enables cross border and domestic exchanges of small, frequent sums of money. For example, as little as $2 (in Ghana Cedis) can be sent to someone in Kenya who receives the equivalent amount in Kenyan Shillings, instantly. **web.chippercash.com**

Margit Uusma – *What's Up Tallinn* brings adventurers, entrepreneurs and professionals to explore Estonian culture, landscape, language and history. **whatsuptallinn.com**

Margit Uusma and Natalie Clark – Matchmaking for expats and digitalnomads at **ExpatMatchmakers.com**

Michael Muniz – *Free Conference*, the first (and best) free conference calling service, enabled me to remain connected with my team while working remotely. Regular online meetings and video conference calls helped me maximize productivity and optimize communication, reducing a distance of thousands of miles to mere milliseconds. **freeconference.com**

Mike Raven – *LEAPS* exists to unite, inspire and accelerate the best of humanity, through People and Innovation. Set up as an international remote start-up. **discoverleaps.com**

Morgan Caracciolo- *AutoCAD Technician* for Transglobal Services, LLC (TGS)-an elite field service provider in the energy industry operating throughout the United States. TGS provides services in land, right-of-way, survey, seismic, and GIS. **www.transgloballlc.com**

Nandita Shetty & Lee Wagner – BestTravelShots.com is a website dedicated to publishing GPS coordinates to the best travel photos worldwide, so you can take the "best shot" while traveling! Website includes featured photos, photographers, travelers, international locations, and tips on how to take (and edit) the best photo from your phone.

Shruti Dwivedi – *Roameasy* connects digital nomads and remote professionals to homes and co-working space before moving to another city or country. Now it's easier to settle in and find friends before you move. **Roameasy.co**

Taylor Christopher - Savage USA was created from two online courses focusing on how to launch an Amazon Private Label (ImportDojo and Jungle Scout). The Savage brand uses sustainable bamboo to build the coolest polarized sunglasses out there at an affordable price! Order yours today! **www.amazon.com/dp/B076G1HQ5D?th=1**

Get loads of FREE STUFF at NiceLife.ca

JOIN REMOTE YEAR

Want to be a digital nomad with Remote Year?
Just send me an email and I'll hook you up with an interview.
janet@nicelife.ca